BLIND DATE

Rogelio Martinez

I0139631

BROADWAY PLAY PUBLISHING INC
New York
www.broadwayplaypublishing.com
info@broadwayplaypublishing.com

BLIND DATE
© Copyright 2022 Rogelio Martinez

Cover art by Mark Bauhs

First edition: May 2022
I S B N: 978-0-88145-926-5

Book design: Marie Donovan
Page make-up: Adobe InDesign
Typeface: Palatino

For my wife, whose trust in my writing resulted in a play whose central theme is trust. A blind date led us both to happiness. And for my children, Charlotte and Miranda.

BLIND DATE was originally commissioned by the Denver Center for the Performing Arts Theatre Company, Kent Thompson, Artistic Director.

BLIND DATE was first produced by the Goodman Theatre in the Albert Theatre in Chicago, running from 20 January-25 February 2018. The cast and creative contributors were:

RONALD REAGAN ....Rob Riley
NANCY REAGAN ....Deanna Dunagan
MIKHAIL GORBACHEV .... William Dick
RAISA GORBACHEV .... Mary Beth Fisher
GEORGE SHULTZ .... Jim Ortlieb
EDUARD SHEVARDNADZE .... Steve Pickering
EDMUND MORRIS.. Thomas J Cox
Ensemble .... Jim Farruggio, Torrey Hanson,
Gregory Linington, Doug McDade,
Michael Milligan, Craig Spidle

Director ....Robert Falls
Scenic design .... Riccardo Hernández
Costume design .... Amy Clark
Lighting Design .... Aaron Spivey
Sound Design ....Richard Woodbury
Dramaturg ....Jonathan L Green
Production Stage Manager .... Briana J Fahey
Stage Manager .... Kimberly Ann McCann

CHARACTERS

GEORGE SHULTZ
EDUARD SHEVARDNADZE
MIKHAIL GORBACHEV
RONALD REAGAN
NANCY REAGAN
RAISA GORBACHEV
EDMUND MORRIS

WAITER, PETER, SOLOMENTSEV, POLITBURO MEMBER,
AIDE, OFFICER, MAJOR, LIEUTENANT COMMANDER,
BILL CASEY, DON REGAN, CASPAR WEINBERGER,
INTELLIGENCE OFFICER, LARRY SPEAKES, REPORTERS,
VYACHESLAV ZAITSEV, AGENT, K G B AGENT

ACT ONE

Scene 1

(A light on GEORGE SHULTZ, *Secretary of State)*

SHULTZ: *(To us)* It wasn't too long ago when letters between world leaders were passed by hand and delivered directly to Heads of State.
March, 1985.
The restaurant was Old Ebbitt Grill a few steps away from the White House. Present was Eduard Shevardnadze, Soviet Minister of Foreign Affairs and myself.
Mr Shevardnadze was a highly educated man, he spoke English, Romanian, and Hungarian.

(A light on EDUARD SHEVARDNADZE*)*

SHEVARDNADZE: *(To us)* And French.
In front of me sat George Shultz, Secretary of State.
He played the role of nice guy but I was not deceived.
Before this he worked in the Nixon White House and did not go to jail. That fact alone told me he was dangerous.

SHULTZ: I recommend ordering it. It's delicious. They call it the Congress Combo. A martini glass for the shrimp; another for your drink.

SHEVARDNADZE: Interesting combo.

SHULTZ: During Prohibition they didn't know what to do with all the martini glasses laying around; so they invented the shrimp cocktail.

SHEVARDNADZE: I never cared for gin.

SHULTZ: Vodkatini? In my younger years it went by the Kangaroo.

SHEVARDNADZE: What is a kangaroo?

SHULTZ: A vodka martini.
Why it was first called that…no one knows. In fact, these days try ordering a Kangaroo and you won't get anywhere.
The bartender here is an old friend. He'd probably know.

SHEVARDNADZE: Americans…sometimes…

SHULTZ: What is it?

SHEVARDNADZE: If it's not your politics, it's names you give to drinks.
You don't understand why you do half the things you do.

SHULTZ: We are working on it.

SHEVARDNADZE: Are you sure?

SHULTZ: There are things that have been in place so long we've stopped questioning them.

(Beat)

SHEVARDNADZE: I agree.

SHULTZ: We're wondering if it's not time we start to question them again.

SHEVARDNADZE: Then you do this for me. You go and find out why vodka martini is called Kangaroo. Find out reason and see if it's possible to even begin to make sense of this.

SHULTZ: *(To us)* I call it gardening.
You plant a garden but if you don't take care of it what do you have?
Weeds.
We'd broken off talks with the Soviets when they first invaded Afghanistan six years earlier. Now the garden was overgrown with weeds.

(By now the WAITER is there.)

WAITER: Mr Shultz?

SHULTZ: The same as always.

WAITER: Good. And you, Sir?

SHEVARDNADZE: Shrimp cocktail.

WAITER: The Congress Combo?

SHEVARDNADZE: I will drink a Manhattan, young man. Jim Beam. Two cherries. One placed on a wooden skewer but the second cherry just let swim freely in the whiskey.

WAITER: Let swim freely in the whiskey.

SHEVARDNADZE: Correct.

(WAITER exits.)

SHEVARDNADZE: They have little to say but then…

SHULTZ: Americans are starting to recycle.

SHEVARDNADZE: What was that?

SHULTZ: We are starting to recycle. Plastic.

SHEVARDNADZE: I have heard this. It is being made mandatory.

SHULTZ: In some States. Yes.

SHEVARDNADZE: And what is the cost if you don't do it.

SHULTZ: A fine.
It's all very new.

SHEVARDNADZE: Some strong-arm tactics do make sense. Would you not agree, Mr Secretary?

SHULTZ: I haven't given it much thought.

SHEVARDNADZE: You should.

(SHULTZ reaches for an envelope but just as he is about to hand it over the WAITER returns with their orders.)

WAITER: Here you are, Mr Secretary.

SHULTZ: Thank you, Jones.

WAITER: And a Manhattan for you.
Two cherries.

SHEVARDNADZE: Jim Beam.

WAITER: As you requested.

SHULTZ: Hold on, Jones. If you don't mind asking Peter to come by when he gets the chance.

WAITER: Have you decided what you are having for lunch, Gentlemen?

SHULTZ: Give us a chance.

(The WAITER goes.)

(The letter remains in SHULTZ's hand…in a kind of no man's land. It's clear SHEVARDNADZE sees the letter. He smiles and then…)

SHEVARDNADZE: Let's eat.

(SHULTZ puts the letter down on his own side of the table.)

SHULTZ: *(To us)* Prior to Princeton I attended Loomis Chaffee School, a college preparatory school. It was there I learned something about the shrimp cocktail. In business and important meetings, you eat it using a small fork. With friends you use your hands. But they made it positively clear.
Make sure these people really are your friends.
Don't risk it.

SHEVARDNADZE: *(To us)* He used his hands. There was a fork but he used his hands.

SHULTZ: *(To us)* I wanted him to believe we were just friends out for a weekly lunch. I wanted to create a certain intimacy between the two of us. A trust.

SHEVARDNADZE: *(To us)* In the Soviet Union when strangers meet for a first lunch we always use fork.

SHULTZ: *(To us)* Once he chose the fork I felt foolish. I had miscalculated his ability to see through me.

SHEVARDNADZE: *(To us)* I was not his friend; but I also did not want to be his enemy. In the spirit of compromise at some point I used my hands.

SHULTZ: *(To us)* Soon we focused our attention on the thing most important to both of us: our grandchildren.

(SHEVARDNADZE places a small photograph on SHULTZ's side of the table...on the letter.)

SHEVARDNADZE: Her name is Sopho. She loves the piano and dance. I believe she has talent but who am I to decide.

SHULTZ: You are her grandfather. That gives you some right to believe in her future.

SHEVARDNADZE: It gives me right to pay for her future. There is this saying in Soviet Union. We must give financial support to our grandchildren until they reach pension age.

SHULTZ: No difference here, I'm afraid.

SHEVARDNADZE: I am one who sees possibility but also the complicated road to get there.
I want a future for her.

SHULTZ: *(To us)* The man was crafty. Was he discussing his granddaughter's dreams or our own future.

(SHEVARDNADZE *picks up the picture and looks at it carefully. Then as if he were addressing the little girl in the picture…*)

SHEVARDNADZE: I feel for her because any noble pursuit always leads to disappointment.

SHULTZ: Not always.

SHEVARDNADZE: It seems that's been the case for a long time.

SHULTZ: *(To us)* We gave equal time to discussing our children, grandchildren, and the fate of the world.
(He takes out an envelope.)
By the way….

SHEVARDNADZE: Ah. I knew there was a by the way. Enough with the suspense, Mr Secretary, you can turn letter over to me now.

SHULTZ: This is to go directly to General Secretary Gorbachev.

SHEVARDNADZE: If you allow me to ask—

SHULTZ: It is a letter from the President congratulating the General Secretary. He knows the times ahead will be difficult but he has faith that—

SHEVARDNADZE: He knows we have difficult times ahead? Does he? If I may. How does he know this?

(At that moment PETER, *a bartender, enters.)*

PETER: What can I do for you, George?

SHULTZ: Peter. The Kangaroo. What's the origin of that?

PETER: The vodka martini.

SHULTZ: That's right. Why was it called that at one time.

PETER: I suppose the vodka, kangaroo connection.

SHULTZ: And what is that connection.

PETER: I have no idea.

(He goes.)

(SHEVARDNADZE reaches for the letter, toys with it, before tucking it away.)

SHEVARDNADZE: *(Smiling)* Kangaroo.

(Beat)

You go and find out about Kangaroo. Come back to me with an answer.

SHULTZ: Fair enough.

SHEVARDNADZE: You do that and I come back with answer.

SHULTZ: Good.

SHEVARDNADZE: The General Secretary will read letter carefully.

SHULTZ: Thank you.

SHEVARDNADZE: I will make sure he gets it and responds promptly.
He will study every single word.

SHULTZ:*(To us)* The letter of congratulations would not have been possible if the Soviets had not taken the first step.

(A light on SOLOMENTSEV, a high-ranking Member of the Soviet Politburo.)

SOLOMENTSEV: It is the spirit of innovation. He prepares for sessions of the Secretariat of the Central Committee and the Politburo really well, introduces new proposals during the discussion of issues, and expresses interesting thoughts. This spirit of innovation is especially valuable. At the same time, he consistently adheres to the course of our party, to its Leninist principles, in his work.

SHULTZ: *(To us)* That was just a small excerpt. He went on for almost an hour. Mikhail Gorbachev was to become the next General Secretary of the Communist Party. The Soviet Politburo had chosen a young man of fifty-four not a geriatric. In the last five years I had attended the funeral of two different General Secretaries.

(Shift)

Scene 2

(Funeral. All over portraits of General Secretary Andropov. Solemn Soviet military music)

(POLITBURO MEMBER enters.)

POLITBURO MEMBER: It is of great honor to us you attend this sad day in Soviet history.

(Sirens, bells, artillery fire all go off at the same time.)

POLITBURO MEMBER: *(Trying to talk over all the noise)* Do not be alarmed. This is Soviet tradition.

SHULTZ: What's that you said?

POLITBURO MEMBER: *(Louder)* Soviet tradition. Loud noise.

SHULTZ: *(Even louder)* How long?

POLITBURO MEMBER: What?

SHULTZ: When will the noise end?

POLITBURO MEMBER: *(Obviously responding to some other question that was never asked)* The State is the Party!

SHULTZ: *(Louder)* I'm sorry?

POLITBURO MEMBER: Yes. We are sorry also. It disappoints us your President could not attend the funeral.

SHULTZ: I will see what I can do for the next one.

POLITBURO MEMBER: Please repeat. I do not understand.

SHULTZ: Same time next year. *(To us)* I was off by a month.

(Shift)

(All over portraits of General Secretary Chernenko. Solemn Soviet military music.)

SHULTZ: *(To us)* This time it was Chernenko. Another very lavish and very expensive funeral. Their economy was in no shape for another one.

POLITBURO MEMBER: We welcome you to this sad occasion. Our people carry heavy hearts full of grief. We are pleased to share these heavy hearts with you.

SHULTZ: *(To us)* Was it me or was their English getting worse?

POLITBURO MEMBER: May I escort you to Chernenko? He waits in coffin.

SHULTZ: I'll be right there. If he can wait just a little longer.

POLITBURO MEMBER: I will make sure he waits.

SHULTZ: *(To us)* It was then that I saw Gorbachev for the very first time. He was off to the side watching. His eyes were on the people stepping forward to pay their final respects to Andropov—excuse me, Chernenko. What was he thinking? Was he trying to figure out who were his allies, enemies. Little by little, people gravitated to him. Near him was a second man with wild, white hair. Eduard Amvrosievich Shevardnadze. Little did I know that a month later the two of us would sit down for lunch.

(An AIDE enters holding a yellow legal pad with notes. She looks down at her notes.)

AIDE: Eduard Amvrosievich Shevardnadze had not been anywhere near our radar. He was the head of the K G B in his native Georgia, but when he became a Party Leader we stopped following him.

SHULTZ: Why?

AIDE: There are close to eight hundred Party Leaders. Too many of them. We don't have the resources.

SHULTZ: It says here, "Eduard Amvrosievich has shown himself as an experienced, resilient person, capable of finding needed approaches to solving problems." What does this mean?

AIDE: It's Gorbachev's own words.

SHULTZ: Needed approaches to solving problems. Problems.

(To us)

In diplomacy, one studies every word carefully. No Soviet leader in recent times had ever used the word problems when describing the conditions of the Soviet State.

AIDE: He's from Georgia.

(Beat)

AIDE: Georgian Soviet Socialist Republic. Birthplace of Stalin.

(SHEVARDNADZE *enters as* AIDE *and* SHULTZ *disappear.*)

SHEVARDNADZE: *(To us)* As head of the K G B, I worked hard to fight corruption, was married, and had two children. And unlike Stalin's children, none have committed suicide.

(Shift)

Scene 3

(A portrait of GORBACHEV *comes down and the General Secretary himself appears holding a letter.)*

GORBACHEV: You want me to say yes to the letter.

SHEVARDNADZE: I want you to understand—

GORBACHEV: Read the letter.

SHEVARDNADZE: I have.

GORBACHEV: The President of the United States is inviting me to come to Washington as if I am in need of some assistance. As if our country is in desperate straits. He's not willing to meet me halfway. Paris. Germany. Come to Washington he writes. Come to us with open hands. He wishes to humiliate me even before...

(Beat)

GORBACHEV: Have you noticed how hot it is in this office? General Secretary Chernenko preferred it be kept that way. I have been here three weeks now and I have not changed the room temperature to my preference.

SHEVARDNADZE: That is the least of your problems.

GORBACHEV: If I wanted to do it I would not even know how.

SHEVARDNADZE: What would you like it to be?

GORBACHEV: Why start to mess with things now. Until I am certain that this is not just a temporary position I will leave things as they are.

SHEVARDNADZE: Even if it means—

GORBACHEV: That I have to take my jacket off. It's the easiest thing to do.

SHEVARDNADZE: Do nothing.

GORBACHEV: You know, Eduard, things have not settled yet. Most of these men around me…they've been walking these halls a lot longer than I have. I sometimes wonder when the knock will come and the movers return.

SHEVARDNADZE: But until that happens—

GORBACHEV: When I chose you as my Foreign Minister I ignored many others ahead of you in line. I can only do so many things before…let's leave it at that.

(SHEVARDNADZE *reads from the letter.*)

SHEVARDNADZE: The letter is not an invitation to come to Washington.

GORBACHEV: That's what it says.

SHEVARDNADZE: He expects you to say no but he also wants to make it clear he's willing to sit across the table from you.

GORBACHEV: Then why isn't he clearer.

SHEVARDNADZE: He has people walking the halls too.

GORBACHEV: You're giving the man too much credit. He's not smart.

SHEVARDNADZE: You shouldn't underestimate him. *(Beat)* Why me?
Why did you choose me to be your Foreign Minister?

GORBACHEV: You were a natural choice.

SHEVARDNADZE: Why?

GORBACHEV: It's obvious, Eduard.

SHEVARDNADZE: My silver hair.

GORBACHEV: You are incorruptible. Honest. Smart.

SHEVARDNADZE: Go on.

GORBACHEV: That's enough.

SHEVARDNADZE: But why me if you have no intention of following my advice.

(Beat)

GORBACHEV: You would tell me the truth.

SHEVARDNADZE: The truth is not good, Misha. The economy is not doing well, morale is down, hope... where has it gone to?

GORBACHEV: I will closely examine our economic—

SHEVARDNADZE: We both have children, grandchildren.

GORBACHEV: You're exhausting.

SHEVARDNADZE: We don't see their flaws and sometimes ignore their bad behavior. Misha, I am the first Foreign Minister born after the birth of the Soviet Union. You are its first General Secretary.
The ones who came before us. Khrushchev, Brezhnev, Chernenko, Andropov—

GORBACHEV: You're missing one.

SHEVARDNADZE: Let's not go there; but these other men...the Soviet Union was their child. They ignored all its problems. Flaws. They could not see the truth even when it was put in front of them. Fortunately, Misha, we can. We can do something about it before it's too late.

GORBACHEV: I can't accept his invitation.

SHEVARDNADZE: You can start a dialogue.

(Beat)

GORBACHEV: The people walking these hallways... they can't know the extent of what I'm doing. We must move slowly.

(SHEVARDNADZE nods yes.)

GORBACHEV: Do you have a piece of paper?

SHEVARDNADZE: Misha, our economy is in such rough shape we can't afford paper.

(GORBACHEV *smiles.*)

GORBACHEV: Go and find some. I will reject his invitation but I will make clear that a dialogue between our two countries is.
Possible?

SHEVARDNADZE: Thank you.

GORBACHEV: Good night.

SHEVARDNADZE: General Secretary, adjust the room temperature to your preference. They will not come knocking any time soon.

(GORBACHEV *goes.*)

SHEVARDNADZE: *(To us)* We were a locomotive going so fast a crash was only a matter of time.

(Shift)

Scene 4

SHULTZ: Three weeks later.

SHEVARDNADZE: *(To us)* Same restaurant.

SHULTZ: *(To us)* I expected a letter in response to the President's invitation; instead, he brought with him a bottle of the finest Russian vodka. We each had a glass. It burned my insides but seemed to have no effect on him.
Then a second glass.

SHEVARDNADZE: How do you enjoy it?

SHULTZ: Very good taste. *(To us)* Acid. Pure acid.

SHEVARDNADZE: And what is this taste you describe?

SHULTZ: It's complicated.

SHEVARDNADZE: Explain this complicated.

SHULTZ: Very full. Rich. Smooth.

(To us)

Acid. Pure acid.

SHEVARDNADZE: Rich? Smooth? Full?

Vodka is not California wine! It is acid!

Pure acid!

Do not believe me to be a fool.

How do I believe a word you say if you can't even tell
me truth about vodka!

(He rises suddenly.)

SHULTZ: Mr Foreign Minister—

SHEVARDNADZE: You think you're so smart. We have
some of the best intelligence in the world. Let me share
one fact with you that the rest of the world does not
know. You can confirm or deny.

Your ass, Mr Secretary, has the tattoo of tiger.

SHULTZ: Excuse me?

SHEVARDNADZE: You have tattoo on ass. True or not.

SHULTZ: *(To us)* How did he know? I have been
investigated by the F B I, the I R S, by the Senate
Intelligence Committee. My mail is opened.
I don't have any secrets left. The only thing I have left,
what is on my rear end.

SHEVARDNADZE: We are smarter than you believe us to
be. We know everything about you.

SHULTZ: You've made that obvious.

SHEVARDNADZE: You pretend to be this polite and
classy man but that's who you are. You carry this great
burden and shame with you.

SHULTZ: Great burden?

SHEVARDNADZE: Mr Secretary, you will not fool us.

SHULTZ: Do you know how I got it? Does your intelligence go that far? Princeton.

The Princeton Tigers.

Mascot?

I have great pride in my school. The same pride I have for my country. I don't have an American flag tattooed on my ass but I have great pride for my country. Its existence. I will not do anything that will bring harm to it. I am not a liar.

(SHEVARDNADZE *turns to go, but is stopped by* SHULTZ's *words.*)

SHULTZ: One day one of the kids must have seen it—not sure how. He spread the word and soon my other children were insisting I show it to them. I said I would. They got very close. Laughing as kids tend to do. And just when I was about to show them...I growled back at them.

RRaaaaaaaaaaHHHHH!

(SHEVARDNADZE *is taken aback.* SHULTZ *takes a third shot.*)

(*A breath...*)

SHULTZ: RRaaaaaaaaaaHHHHH!

SHEVARDNADZE: Secretary Shultz, I warn you. Slow down on that vodka there. As American television states, It's the Real Thing.

(SHEVARDNADZE *hands* SHULTZ *a letter and exits.*)

Scene 5

(REAGAN *along with military brass.*)

(*The group stands over a leather briefcase holding a computer inside.*)

OFFICER: Go ahead.

REAGAN: These numbers here…

OFFICER: Yes. Followed by that second set.

(REAGAN reaches inside his jacket looking for something but when he can't find what he is looking for he turns to an OFFICER.)

REAGAN: May I use yours?

(A moment of confusion before the OFFICER realizes what REAGAN is asking for.)

REAGAN: Thank you.

Now if this was real and this young man was not here what would happen?

(Pause)

All right. I'll make sure to always carry a pair.
What happens next?

OFFICER: There are five final numbers.

REAGAN: And then?

OFFICER: At best fifteen minutes between when we launch our missiles and they begin a counterstrike.

REAGAN: And afterwards?

OFFICER: Another ten minutes and that would be all.

REAGAN: When you say that will be all.

OFFICER: Yes.

REAGAN: And if a mistake was made. No reading glasses, wrong translation, a drunk sailor.

(The officers smile…was this last statement a joke? NO.)

OFFICER: Let's go on, Mr President. The final five numbers. When you're ready.
When you're ready, Sir.

REAGAN: And you're sure this is just a test.

OFFICER: Yes.

REAGAN: Last chance?

OFFICER: It's a test.

(In complete silence, REAGAN punches in the codes. One final code and the room remains silent.)

REAGAN: And now?

MAJOR: You have fifteen minutes from when you punch in that last set of numbers to stand down.

REAGAN: These letters and numbers here is the code to stand down?

MAJOR: No. That there launches a nuclear—

REAGAN: Oh.

MAJOR: These other numbers—

REAGAN: And if I were to make a mistake when standing down.

MAJOR: One single mistake would indicate that your orders to stand down are false. At that point things would go forward as planned.

REAGAN: One mistake on my part and then…

LIEUTENANT COMMANDER: At best fifteen minutes between when we launch our missiles and they begin a counterstrike.
(Beat)
At best.

REAGAN: And afterwards?

MAJOR: Another ten minutes and that would be all.

REAGAN: When you say that would be all.

(Pause)

LIEUTENANT COMMANDER: That would be all. Yes. Sir.

(Light on SHULTZ)

SHULTZ: *(To us)* Imagine that. One mistake and there would be no way to avert nuclear war. The President would later explain to me just how profoundly affected he was by this one idea. One mistake on either side and there would be no turning back. This one idea would haunt him long after he left office.

Scene 6

(SHULTZ, REAGAN, GORBACHEV *and* SHEVARDNADZE)

SHULTZ: *(To us)* Soon after Gorbachev rejected Reagan's invitation, they began to exchange letters.

SHEVARDNADZE: The President's letters were written longhand, in a childlike script.

SHULTZ: The General Secretary's letters were typed on a 1983 Lyubava typewriter.

(During the following, images of the letters flow across the stage.)

SHEVARDNADZE: *(To us)* April 30.

GORBACHEV: I think a lot about the shape the affairs between our countries can take. Of course, our countries are different and this fact will not change

SHULTZ: *(To us)* May 5.

REAGAN: I could not agree more with your statement that each social system—capitalism or communism—should prove its advantages not by force but by peaceful competition. All people have the right to go their chosen way without imposition from the other side.

SHEVARDNADZE: *(To us)* May 16.

GORBACHEV: We impose neither our ideology, nor our social system on anybody. Please do not ascribe to us what does not exist. And what about direct pressure on the government whose policy does not suit the U S? There are enough examples of your country doing that.

SHULTZ: *(To us)* It was then that the President decided to go silent.

(SHEVARDNADZE appears.)

SHEVARDNADZE: *(To us)* The result was that the General Secretary became even more confrontational.

GORBACHEV: Dear Mr President.

SHULTZ: *(To us)* What followed was a series of issues Gorbachev found of grave concern. Grave concern. His words.

GORBACHEV: We have proposed that any work on anti-missile systems be confined to laboratories. In response we witness attempts to justify the development of space weapons…

SHULTZ: *(To us)* General Secretary Gorbachev's chief complaint now centered around S D I—Strategic Defense Initiative. The President wanted to put satellites up in space capable of destroying nuclear weapons before they reached their targets.

SHEVARDNADZE: *(To us)* The media had jokingly referred to the President's idea using the name of a very successful film that had inspired two sequels. I had only seen the second film in which an evil empire strikes back.

SHULTZ: *(To us)* The media's glibness clearly showed how accustomed the American people had become to an earlier acronym—MAD.

SHEVARDNADZE: *(To us)* Mutual Assured Destruction. MAD.
You blow us up; we blow you up. One of the most terrifying, brilliant ideas mankind had come up with.

SHULTZ: *(To us)* The idea behind MAD made sense…as long as the people in charge were not mad themselves; but both the President and I feared one day we'd have a madman for President.

GORBACHEV: I would note that on several occasions we have explicitly expressed our views on the American program of developing space attack weapons and a large scale anti-ballistic missile system. I stress once again. The implementation of this program will not solve the problem of nuclear arms, it will only aggravate it and have the most negative consequences. Should the United States rush with weapons into space we would do our utmost to stop it.

(And with that, GORBACHEV *is gone.)*

SHULTZ: Mr President.

REAGAN: George.

SHULTZ: I want you to entertain this idea.

REAGAN: I'm ready to be entertained, but you're a smart man and I know what you're going to say.

SHULTZ: You must meet the General Secretary face to face.

REAGAN: You have him there in that letter in front of you, George.
What is there to meet about?

SHULTZ: What is written down on paper does not always match up with how the person really feels. Mr President, there is only one way to know for sure what he really believes.

REAGAN: Politics, George. It's how it all works.

SHULTZ: Mr President.

REAGAN: You're not going to give up, are you?

SHULTZ: The American people gave you a four-picture deal. They were generous enough to renew the contract.

REAGAN: Now that's clever.

SHULTZ: You can do this because after these four years, you're being retired.
(To us)
I couldn't get him to change his mind.
And then things got more difficult.

(Shift)

Scene 7

(Oval Office)

(REAGAN, SHULTZ, and BILL CASEY, head of the C I A, are there.)

BILL: They come to our country as international civil servants, but they have always been a counterintelligence problem.
Gennadi Fyodorovich Zakharov is a physicist by day and a spy by day *and* night.

SHULTZ: Are you certain?

BILL: I think it's the President that needs to ask the questions.

REAGAN: Are you certain?

BILL: Because the United Nations does not work closely with us, it's almost impossible to put any kind of control on these people.
We got lucky with Zakharov.
We'd been on him for a while and finally caught him doing a dead drop.

SHULTZ: You said you'd been on him for a while.

BILL: That's right.

SHULTZ: What's a while?

BILL: A while.

REAGAN: How long?

BILL: A year and a half.

SHULTZ: You couldn't snag him earlier.
That's a lot of time and resources, Bill.
When you have your eyes on him, it shouldn't go
longer than six months.

BILL: Let me do my job and you do yours.
(Turning to REAGAN)
Mr President, the Soviets have a long tradition of
dispatching civil servants in pursuit of a greater goal.
They are here and we don't have enough resources or
support to do what we have to do.

SHULTZ: Are you here informing us that you have a
Soviet spy under custody, or are you here asking for a
budget increase.

REAGAN: Thank you, Bill.

BILL: George, rumor has it you're involved in some sort
of backroom talks.
You ought to be careful. These guys are crafty
motherfuckers.
I'm sorry, Mr President.

(BILL goes. REAGAN returns to his papers.)

REAGAN: You insist on a face to face, but I can't do it,
George. It's not the right time.

(Shift)

Scene 8

(Old Ebbitt Grill)

*(*Shultz *is at his regular table when* Shevardnadze *enters.)*

Shevardnadze: Hello, George.

Shultz: Eduard, it's not good to be late.

Shevardnadze: I was busy booking my ticket back to Moscow. Aisle seat.

Shultz: The President is very concerned about the arresting of an American journalist—

Shevardnadze: We're concerned you arrested this young physicist.

Shultz: Soviet spy.

Shevardnadze: That's your belief.

Shultz: The President also met with the journalist's family.
As you know, President Reagan is a man who can be led by his emotions. He was very upset after he met Daniloff's daughter.

Shevardnadze: Gennadi Zakharov also has a family. Three children. They want him home.

Shultz: Gennadi Zakharov is a spy. We know this for a fact.
Your arrest of an innocent American journalist is just a sad excuse for you to retaliate.

(A breath)

Shultz: I can't do this alone, Eduard. As it stands, the President is holding firm.

Shevardnadze: There will be other opportunities.

Shultz: The C I A has had their eye on Zakharov for a year. They chose to arrest him now. Why?

There are people in the Cabinet who want nothing more than to convince the President now is not the right time for talks. Your actions are playing right into their hands.

SHEVARDNADZE: I am sorry, George. I have two hours to get to airport. I have one suitcase and a briefcase stuffed with bad news.

SHULTZ: Zakharov is a spy; Daniloff is not.

SHEVARDNADZE: This investigation continues. We cannot share this information because there may be others. We will share it at a future time.

SHULTZ: You are playing a very dangerous game. We can lose it all if we go down this silly road.

(SHEVARDNADZE *looks all around the room.*)

SHEVARDNADZE: This is a lousy restaurant.
Why do you insist on bringing me here every time?
Rude staff and mediocre food, but there is not one table empty.
Is there a reason for that?

SHULTZ: Power.
All these people have something to do with power.
It may be a bad restaurant but there's not one person here willing to make that first move and stop coming.
We are trapped.
After I leave office I will never set foot here again; but right now I have one of the better tables.
Is that clear?
Let me be clearer.
I have the best table here. And you're sitting across from me. At the best table. We have the greatest influence on the two that can change it all.
We may be ruining our last chance even before we've started.

(Pause)

SHEVARDNADZE: I have already shared this concern with the General Secretary.

SHULTZ: What was his response?

SHEVARDNADZE: The West likes Gorbachev. Maybe it's because he seems a reasonable man. I don't know. What I do know is that the Soviet Politburo is not so happy with that. He has to show a sign of strength. Give us Zakharov and maybe we can find a future for our grandchildren.

(Pause)

SHULTZ: Release Daniloff to the American embassy in an hour's time; and book him a flight out of Moscow no later than tomorrow afternoon. Eight days from now when the world is looking the other way we will do the same.

SHEVARDNADZE: You don't have that authority.

SHULTZ: I've already told you. I have the best table here.

(Beat)

SHEVARDNADZE: Your President must not take any credit for Daniloff's release.
He must stop being a politician and let this one go quietly. If the President even suggests he's responsible, then he will have proved himself untrustworthy.
Do I have the President's word?

SHULTZ: You do.

SHEVARDNADZE: One more thing.
The General Secretary will announce Zakharov's return. He will take full credit for it. His popularity at home will grow and it will buy him time.
This time around the General Secretary needs to be the politician.

Okey dokey?

(SHULTZ *nods yes.*)

SHULTZ: *(To us)* We brought home an American.

SHEVARDNADZE: *(To us)* We brought home a spy. Now who won that round?

(From his suitcase, SHULTZ now pulls out several newspapers.)

SHEVARDNADZE: Ah, *Pravda*!

SHULTZ: Truth.
Anything but truth.

SHEVARDNADZE: We have a terrific subscription plan, George. Free for life.

SHULTZ: *(To us)* George. He called me by my first name. The world changed at that moment.
(To SHEVARDNADZE)
I'm afraid I can't take you up on that subscription offer.

SHEVARDNADZE: Oh, shame.

SHULTZ: I'm already a subscriber. I enjoy the fiction. Now look closely.

SHEVARDNADZE: May I.

(SHULTZ hands over the newspaper.)

SHEVARDNADZE: Ah. Confirm. The good-looking man standing near the General Secretary is me.

SHULTZ: In all these pictures of the General Secretary there seems to be one thing missing.

SHEVARDNADZE: What is that, George?

SHULTZ: Nevus flammeus.

SHEVARDNADZE: Afraid my English does not go so far as to understand this word.

SHULTZ: They call it a port-wine stain.

SHEVARDNADZE: I need more help.

SHULTZ: A birthmark near the right side of his forehead.

(SHEVARDNADZE *studies it.*)

SHULTZ: The Kremlin allows for the one newspaper. As you can see, the General Secretary—

SHEVARDNADZE: Let's do away with formalities. Call him Misha.

SHULTZ: Misha.

SHEVARDNADZE: Yes, Misha.
And you allow me to call your President Ronnie.

SHULTZ: As you can see Misha is only photographed from the left side. In those rare instances where he is photographed straight on they remove his birthmark.

SHEVARDNADZE: How interesting.
Coincidence.

SHULTZ: We would like you to stop this coincidence, Eduard. As a sign that the Soviet Union is willing to open up—

SHEVARDNADZE: Open up?

SHULTZ: Glasnost.
To show you mean what you say, show the world the whole of the General Secretary.

SHEVARDNADZE: *(To us)* A small request. Why not?

SHULTZ: *(To us)* My request appeared small but I was changing Soviet policy.

SHEVARDNADZE: Okay, George.

Now that we are friends again...between friends only. You will tell me the truth. Your President's hair—

SHULTZ: It's real.

SHEVARDNADZE: Not a wig?

SHULTZ: No.

SHEVARDNADZE: I hear hormone injections.

SHULTZ: Brylcreem. It's pomade.

SHEVARDNADZE: Pomade?

SHULTZ: A styling cream that gives the hair a slightly wet look. We've tried to convince him to stop using it but he won't. The First Lady insists on it.

SHEVARDNADZE: I don't believe you.
His hair is black? Completely black.
No. It is dyed.

SHULTZ: Nyet.

SHEVARDNADZE: Ah good. And the word for yes?

SHULTZ: Da.

SHEVARDNADZE: Congratulations on passing your first lesson.
(He rises.)
Geneva, let us meet halfway.
(He starts to walk away.)

SHULTZ: That's not halfway.

SHEVARDNADZE: You have so much to teach us, George.

SHULTZ: *(To us)* That afternoon I may have partially surrendered the secret to the President's slicked black hair, but when I debriefed him later he supported my decision with that great smile of his.
Next day's edition of *Pravda* published the very first pictures of the General Secretary and his nevus flammeus. As was their custom, the picture carried with it no explanation as to why it hadn't been shown before. One moment it was not there, the next it had appeared.
You decide who won.
(Shift)

Scene 9

(The Oval Office)

(REAGAN sits alone, he looks different. More worried. A thinking man. A knock on the door)

REAGAN: If you must.

(DON REGAN, White House Chief of Staff, enters. REAGAN's demeanor changes. This is the public REAGAN, affable and with a no worries look on his face.)

DON: I got them waiting.

REAGAN: Guests for lunch. Mother asks her youngest to say the blessing.
I don't know what to say?
The mother tries to help: Just say what you heard me say.
Kid bows his head.
"Oh Lord why did I invite these people."
Ever heard that one?

(Quick light shift)

(CASPAR WEINBERGER and SHULTZ are there. Also with them is an INTELLIGENCE OFFICER.)

(We are already into the scene.)

WEINBERGER: Before you decide to meet with the Soviets I just want to tell you they're a bunch of alcoholics.

SHULTZ: *(To us)* Caspar Weinberger, Secretary of Defense. A hawk.

WEINBERGER: They're alcoholics.
On a good day thirty-five percent of the people show up to work with another five percent stumbling in later in the morning.
You know what the best job in the Soviet Union is?
Sweepers. You know what they are?

SHULTZ: No, Cap, we don't but I'm sure you're about
to tell us.

WEINBERGER: Sweepers. Every morning they go
around picking drunks off the street and drive them
home. When the Soviets brag about social services
and kindness and human rights that's what they're
referring to.
Mr President, their shelves are empty. There is nothing
to buy because they're not making anything.
The hospitals are crowded.
Someone sees a line somewhere they get right on it
before even knowing what it's for hoping for what…
hoping for anything.
What are they doing while they wait?

SHULTZ: They're drinking.

WEINBERGER: Princeton boy has it right.
Now if a summit were to take place…well a point for
their side.
Success for him is just getting you to the table.
Go ahead.

SHULTZ: Go on.

INTELLIGENCE OFFICER: The Secretary is correct. All he
wants is recognition. For the world to know he is in
charge and our equal.
It would be a mistake, I believe, to assume the General
Secretary needs a Summit in order to achieve his
domestic goals. The basic resource allocation decisions
for the next several years almost certainly have been
set. Now it is true the Soviet Union had a difficult time
in the 1970s.

REAGAN: Carter.
Carter managed to screw up two countries.

INTELLIGENCE OFFICER: Even a low rate of procurement growth would still enable them to achieve substantial modernization.

In order to meet his goals he is not dependent on arms control.

There is only one thing he really wants.

If a Summit were to occur, the General Secretary will confront you with the threat that no future meetings will take place unless there is a prospect of achieving concrete results.

REAGAN: Which are?

INTELLIGENCE OFFICER: Stop any work on the Strategic Defense Initiative.

WEINBERGER: If you were to say no, he would paint you as a warmonger. He's setting up a trap.

(Beat)

DON: Anything else?

INTELLIGENCE OFFICER: A more thorough report of our findings is contained in this folder for you to study whenever you wish.

(It's a thick folder. REAGAN sets it aside. It's clear he will never read it.)

(WEINBERGER opens the door letting DON and analysts go. It's now SHULTZ, REAGAN, and WEINBERGER.)

WEINBERGER: Alcoholics.

SHULTZ: You're back to that? Let's talk about it because Cap is leaving one important detail out.

WEINBERGER: Go ahead.

SHULTZ: Gorbachev is already addressing this problem—

WEINBERGER: Prohibition. Or whatever the Soviets want to call—

SHULTZ: Let me finish.

WEINBERGER: He's pulling vodka off the shelves. He's forcing the population to give up alcohol. Is that right? Is that what you were referring to, George?

(SHULTZ *nods yes.*)

WEINBERGER: Prohibition. What George is calling prohibition. It's just making him less popular by the minute. There's a joke going around.

In Moscow there's a vodka shortage; so there is a very long line just to be able to buy one bottle. The men in line begin to complain and then one man has a brilliant idea.

I am going to go and complain directly to the General Secretary! Ten minutes go by and he comes back. All his friends want to know what Gorbachev had to say. "I gave up. The line there was even longer!"

(Beat)

WEINBERGER: I think it's very funny. Very enlightening.

REAGAN: You need to work on your delivery, but the point is clear.

WEINBERGER: The hit their economy is taking because of drunkenness is close to sixty billion rubles.

But you cut down on vodka production as the General Secretary is doing then their economy really starts to stall. Overall retail trade goes down five billion rubles yearly. By 1990 they're losing twenty billion. What happens to their military budget? They start to cut it. Soon we have the upper hand.

Theirs is a drunken economy. If they stop drinking the country goes under, but if they continue drinking the country goes under.

Either way you look at it the Soviet Union has about five years left, maybe six.

SHULTZ: Mr President, there's a good chance that Cap is right. And that's what scares me most of all.

I remind you, all it takes is one nuclear launch from them and the world ends.

We need to engage with these people and we need to do it quickly. We need to help them transition…bring them closer to our side. If we sit on this and wait for them to sober up and notice just how bad things really are then…

WEINBERGER: No need for a summit.

A year. Let's see where they are in a year.

SHULTZ: When you back someone into a corner you don't know what they're capable of doing until they do it.

Mr President, we must get ourselves out of this nuclear mess we've gotten ourselves into.

REAGAN: Good. Thank you.
(Pointing over at the folder)
It's always useful to know where a friend or enemy is, whether you want him or whether you don't.
(He rises.)
Make yourselves at home.
(He goes.)

WEINBERGER: What the hell did he just say?!

SHULTZ: It's from Winnie the Pooh.

WEINBERGER: Winnie the Pooh? How the hell would you know that?

SHULTZ: I happened to be reading it to my grandchild.

WEINBERGER: Winnie the Pooh!?

SHULTZ: But the correct quote is, "It's always useful to know where a friend-and-relation is, whether you want him or whether you don't."
(Beat)

His makes more sense.

WEINBERGER: Goodbye, George. I'll see you around the office.

(He exits.)

(Shift)

Scene 10

(The restaurant. SHULTZ *at bar without a jacket.)*

SHULTZ: *(To us)* It was a snowstorm. By that afternoon two inches had fallen. Snow in early October. Unprecedented. It put all of Washington in a panic.

(The bartender, PETER, *has entered, martini glass in hand.)*

PETER: Last call.

SHULTZ: Two is enough.

PETER: Thought you might want it.

SHULTZ: I've had enough.

PETER: Can I put an order in? We're closing the kitchen early.

SHULTZ: I'm fine. Thank you, Peter.

PETER: Find anything out?

SHULTZ: What's that?

PETER: That kangaroo business? Anything.

SHULTZ: No.

PETER: You know what I think it is? After the war, vodka became more popular so people started hopping over from gin to vodka. Hop hop kangaroo.
(Beat)
Oh come on. Not even a smile. What you need to do: you need to get the C I A involved.

SHULTZ: They're busy.

PETER: I mean it. Let's get to the bottom of this. You promised that man I've seen you with an answer.

SHULTZ: I did.

PETER: You gave him your word.

SHULTZ: When you're in my kind of business you break promises.

PETER: A gentleman like yourself?

SHULTZ: I'm not sure government is the right line of work for me anymore.

PETER: Well…we're hiring.

(SHULTZ *pushes the empty glass away from him.* PETER *exits.* SHULTZ *leaves money on bar. Stands up. Puts his coat on.* PETER *returns.*)

PETER: Mr Secretary, you have a phone call.

SHULTZ: Who is it?

PETER: A lady. It's not your wife. A little more… assertive.

(NANCY REAGAN *appears.*)

NANCY: George?

(SHULTZ *steps into his own light.*)

SHULTZ: *(To us)* Not exactly the President but well…

NANCY: George, it's Nancy. We thought maybe you'd like to join us for dinner.

SHULTZ: Of course. Thank you. When?

NANCY: Right now.
(*She is gone.*)

SHULTZ: *(To us)* What did she want? Nancy didn't pick up the phone and invite you to dinner unless she was interested in something. And this something always had to do with the President's standing.

(Shift)

Scene 11

(The East Wing)

NANCY: I prefer this room for after dinner. Staying at the table while the staff clears things. Well it just feels wrong. Leave them to do their work.

SHULTZ: I just wanted to say just how special your meatloaf is.

NANCY: Are you telling me the truth?

SHULTZ: No matter how many times I have it—

NANCY: You didn't think it was a little too salty tonight?

SHULTZ: Not at all

NANCY: You're not tired of it?

SHULTZ: Absolutely not.

NANCY: Oh good. You see my husband tells me the truth about everything but my cooking. Of course, I don't really do much cooking nowadays but when the President of the United States tells you to make meatloaf, George, you do it.

SHULTZ: *(To us)* You will never understand just how nervous Nancy Reagan could make you feel.

NANCY: I'm just glad to have you here on such short notice. We were going to spend the weekend in Camp David but then the snow came.

SHULTZ: Mrs Reagan, where is the President?

NANCY: When you live in a house this size it's not surprising to me when people get lost.

SHULTZ: I don't ever remember being in this room.

NANCY: This was a bedroom once. President Johnson's bed was over in that corner. He had meetings in here with Ladybird sleeping next to him. Can you imagine that? Oh God.

SHULTZ: I do remember now. Dick kept it a bedroom when he came into the White House.

NANCY: There was so much to do when we moved in. It took me almost four years to set things straight. The press doesn't understand but the White House belongs not just to us but to all Americans. It's how we see ourselves. When we moved in it was no more than a fraternity house. I found a peanut butter sandwich in one of the upstairs closets. I'm not saying the Carters— who knows how long that gross thing had been there. And the half-empty beer can. I know Betty Ford had her problems but at the very least she could have finished the can.

SHULTZ: It is a nice house.
(To us)
I was certain we weren't there to discuss the poor living conditions but I couldn't stop her.

NANCY: No matching china. For our first state dinner we hosted Margaret Thatcher. Later when we were alone she hugged me. Real compassion, George. She understood just how embarrassed I was at that moment. Margaret Thatcher hugged me, George.

SHULTZ: Well I think you've done a splendid—

NANCY: You know the outside hadn't been painted in years. How could it be a white house if it's not white.

SHULTZ: *(To us)* And then the room went quiet. I didn't know what to say.

(NANCY takes a breath. Smiles. Stillness)

NANCY: This is nice.

SHULTZ: Yes.

NANCY: Not the snowstorm. Having you here. It seems things have come to a sudden stop.

SHULTZ: What do you mean?

NANCY: The snow, George. It seems no one can get around. Not sure how you made it. I'm glad you did though.

SHULTZ: It was just a walk over. I wasn't far.

NANCY: I know that, George. I called you, remember?

SHULTZ: That's what I was meaning to ask. How did you know where I was?

NANCY: Oh, George…

SHULTZ: *(To us)* She had a wonderful way of avoiding any question she didn't wish to answer.

NANCY: George, ten years from now where do you see us all?

SHULTZ: Alive I hope.

NANCY: This is a serious question. I finally had a chance to read Mr Gorbachev's letters to my husband that you sent me. He can be a very unpleasant man.

SHULTZ: He does have a temper.

NANCY: Does he have a sense of humor?

SHULTZ: As far as…I don't know. I don't think we'd find anything the General Secretary of the Communist Party would say very funny.

NANCY: My husband came to me earlier today with a decision he was being asked to make.

SHULTZ: He's made the decision. He's going to break off talks.

NANCY: Oh, George.

SHULTZ: Yes?

NANCY: I want the world to recognize what we're doing here.

SHULTZ: We?

NANCY: My husband. What my husband is doing.

SHULTZ: Nothing. You can't find your way to common ground if you're not sitting down with the other party.

NANCY: Do you believe the future is something we can predict, George?

SHULTZ: If the right intelligence is in place we can figure it out. Anticipate it.

NANCY: We can all study the past and even make sense of it but the future....

SHULTZ: It can certainly be more challenging.

NANCY: My husband is a man who finds confrontation upsetting. Not on the world stage but...well we had to tie him down to a chair and pick up the phone before he finally fired the last person to hold your job.

(Pause)

SHULTZ: Mrs Reagan, am I being fired.

NANCY: Of course not, George.

SHULTZ: Why am I here right now?

NANCY: Why are we anywhere at any moment?

SHULTZ: You're asking me?

NANCY: Why was my husband walking out of a hotel when that man decided to pull out a gun and shoot him? If I had known that young man would be there waiting then my husband would not have had to go through everything he did.
(Pause)
What I say next will never be repeated.

SHULTZ: Fair.

NANCY: Joan believes a summit is the right course of action.

SHULTZ: Joan. Who is Joan?

(Beat)

NANCY: She's my astrologer.

SHULTZ: Excuse me?

NANCY: Absolute discretion, George.

SHULTZ: You said astrologer.

NANCY: She lives in California.

SHULTZ: Joan?

NANCY: Yes, Joan. I talk to her often.

SHULTZ: Astrologer.

NANCY: Yes. My husband is in favor of a summit but there is one little problem that I've discussed with Joan…let me get to the point. The meeting can take place in Geneva. But. George, it must not take place in late October when Mercury is in retrograde. The consequences would be terrible and my husband would not be able to speak coherently. It must happen in mid-November. Can you pull that off, George?

SHULTZ: *(To us)* She was a piece of work but God bless Nancy Reagan.

We moved forward.

The choice of dates—November 19 and the 20th—were proposed by the President who had in turn received them from his wife, who had in turn received them from astrologer Joan Quigley.

(Shift)

Scene 12

(Lights snap up. REPORTERS *swarm the White House Press Room.)*

*(*LARRY SPEAKES, *acting Press Secretary, enters.)*

SPEAKES: Now look at you all bright eyed and bushy tailed. I feel like I'm in a first grade classroom. All right. In front of you is the President's schedule for the day. Are there any questions?

FIRST REPORTER: There's nothing on the piece of paper.

SPEAKES: God I can't get anything past you.

That's because he has nothing planned. Now that second piece of paper there is a statement from Tass regarding the upcoming Geneva Summit. If you want to know what the Soviets have to say about it don't ask me just look at what their news agency has to say about it in their own newspaper.

SECOND REPORTER: In the past you've been quoted as saying anything Pravda prints must not be believed.

SPEAKES: Any country going around with one newspaper—*Pravda*—Truth—and one news agency… well you have to be a little suspect.

FIRST REPORTER: Larry, I'm looking at this document and it's in Russian.

SPEAKES: You expect them to write it in English?

FIRST REPORTER: I'd expect you to share the translation given to the President.

SPEAKES: Your expectations are too high. All you're going to learn is that on November 19th and the 20th the President of the United States and the General Secretary will meet in Geneva.

THIRD REPORTER: That's all the statement says? But it's a page long.

SPEAKES: And War and Peace is a thousand pages. I can't teach them how to write. Look; you're lookin' for a story when there ain't one. For the first time in a while the Russians and the Americans are sitting down to talk. The President is interested in discussing arms reduction. That's it.

FOURTH REPORTER: How does the President feel about nuclear war?

SPEAKES: He's eager to get it started.

Come on. What kind of question is that, Helen. How do *you* feel about nuclear war?

FIFTH REPORTER: In the past the President has made some incendiary remarks—

SPEAKES: And one Soviet leader took off his shoe and banged it on a podium.

FIFTH REPORTER: The President referred to the Soviets as the evil empire.

SPEAKES: The Soviets promised to bury us. Look; they dish it out just as much—and maybe even more—than we do.

THIRD REPORTER: Well this obsession with the destruction—

SPEAKES: Now, we're here to discuss a Summit not nuclear war. When the time comes for nuclear war and if time allows it I'll stand here and be the first one to answer all your questions. Boys, you're all smart people so ask smart questions. Next.

FOURTH REPORTER: Larry—

SPEAKES: Boys and girls. I stand corrected. Go on.

FOURTH REPORTER: There is great anxiety. The world is concerned that nuclear war—

SPEAKES: You won't let it go, Helen. Now understand this. The President has no interest—everybody hearing me—no interest in using nuclear weapons now or in the future. In fact, the Soviets have a greater nuclear arsenal. Those figures have been made available for some time now.

SECOND REPORTER: I've looked at those figures and the math doesn't add up.

SPEAKES: Then use a calculator. Next question.

THIRD REPORTER: What's going to happen when the two leaders meet?

SPEAKES: I'm not a fortune teller. I know the present. I know what the President said. He took me aside and said, The world breathes easier because we are talking together.

FOURTH REPORTER: You and the President or the President and the General Secretary?

SPEAKES: I think it's safe to say yes.

FIRST REPORTER: Hold on a moment, Larry, can we say with any certainty the Summit will go on as planned.

SPEAKES: God willing and the creek don't rise.
Any additional questions can be directed at my office. You'll no doubt get a busy signal but you can always try.
In a week's time you'll get a little package with all the necessary information. All the places you might want to visit while you're in Geneva. I've heard they have a terrific lake y'all can go jump in.

(Shift)

Scene 13

(A bedroom. VYACHESLAV ZAITSEV, *a fashion designer, is there. Flamboyant as one can be under a communist dictatorship,* ZAITSEV *wears a button down suit with a pink pocket square that is very visible.)*

RAISA: *(Off)* Are you ready?

ZAITSEV: Ready, Mrs Gorbachev.

*(*RAISA *enters in a somewhat unappealing outfit.)*

RAISA: Now how does this outfit look?

ZAITSEV: Frumpy.

RAISA: Oh good.

ZAITSEV: Old-fashioned and unremarkable.

RAISA: I think you're right.

ZAITSEV: You look like a housewife.

RAISA: A schoolteacher?

ZAITSEV: Of Marxist philosophy.

RAISA: A bore.

ZAITSEV: To put it mildly.

RAISA: Invisible.

*(*ZAITSEV *nods, then smiles.)*

RAISA: Oh, Slava, you're so good at what you do.

ZAITSEV: I will tell you that the task you gave me was hard. Making someone look fashionable is easy for me but dowdy and well...ugly when you're so stunning. Impossible!

RAISA: You've done your job. I will wear this for the official photo that Pravda will print from the Summit. This is the way the Soviet people want to see me. Let's start working on the way I want the West to see me.

I want three outfits for each day that I'm there. Let's begin modestly; but, of course, you will save your best for the final dinner. Now measure me again.

ZAITSEV: I did it two weeks ago.

RAISA: Do it.

(ZAITSEV *takes out his measuring tape.*)

RAISA: Any change?

ZAITSEV: None whatsoever, Mrs Gorbachev.

RAISA: Good. I intend to stay the only General Secretary's wife to weigh less than her husband.

ZAITSEV: You'll be fine. You have a long way to go.

RAISA: Let's go on.

ZAITSEV: I have something special in mind.

RAISA: Avoid the color red.

ZAITSEV: I believe Mrs Reagan will do the same. As a way to surprise you.

RAISA: Then let's surprise her.

ZAITSEV: That's what I intend to do. Once Mrs Reagan sees what you're wearing she will demand to meet me.

RAISA: And what will you tell her when you sit across from her?

ZAITSEV: (*Obviously having good fun*) I will tell her to defect.

RAISA: You will what?

ZAITSEV: Yes, come to Moscow and get in line.

RAISA: Defection. That would be very embarrassing.

ZAITSEV: Vanity makes people do strange things.

(Beat)

RAISA: Slava, you understand just how important you are to all the changes my husband is trying to achieve.

(Pause)

ZAITSEV: The General Secretary is interested in fashion?

RAISA: Fashion *is* politics. You understand.

*(*ZAITSEV *doesn't.)*

*(*RAISA *pauses to check herself out in the mirror.)*

RAISA: If my husband is to succeed then the West needs to see us as people capable of breaking away from the past. They need to see me. To really see me.

ZAITSEV: That is clear.

RAISA: Did you know that Mrs Brezhnev never once travelled with her husband abroad.

ZAITSEV: No one knows if she is even still alive. Is she?

RAISA: Was she ever alive, Slava. How do you like these colors on me. And lie if you must criticism will not help you.

ZAITSEV: Beautiful.
There's a lot to do and only two weeks to the summit but I will do it. Then when we're there I will stand ready to do anything you ask of me.

RAISA: I know you will.

ZAITSEV: And these colors?

RAISA: You are the artist.

*(*ZAITSEV *walks back to the bed and looks through the different fabrics. Eventually he will make his way back to* RAISA.*)*

RAISA: You know, Slava, I never owned a coat till I was eighteen. When I left for university, my father presented me with one and the whole village came to see it.

ZAITSEV: You've come so far.

RAISA: *(She is now lost in thought, maybe less present in the room than she is in her own mind)* But have we really?
(Beat)
When I go back and read Marx, Lenin...this hardship was not what they dreamed for us. If they could come back for one day, walk the streets, what would they think. I would be ashamed but I would get down on my knees and beg them to come back in ten years to see what we've accomplished.

(Pause)

ZAITSEV: Mrs Gorbachev.

RAISA: How does it feel to have to be two people?

ZAITSEV: I don't understand.

RAISA: Of course you do.

(Beat)

ZAITSEV: There is the public self and the private. One day soon they will be one and the same.

RAISA: I have to believe that but sometimes it's hard. Our country is begging for change but I still have to be the General Secretary's wife who disappears behind her husband. They don't want to see a woman as an equal. The sad thing is that it's not just the men but maybe even more, the women.

ZAITSEV: It will take some time.

RAISA: How long? And will I still be here to enjoy it.
(Beat)
I am sorry, Slava.

ZAITSEV: For what?

RAISA: I can't take you to Geneva with me.

(ZAITSEV puts down the fabric.)

ZAITSEV: Why are you doing this?

RAISA: This is history. If one thing were to go wrong.
One embarrassment.

ZAITSEV: Defection? I was joking.

RAISA: As you say, vanity makes people do strange
things.

ZAITSEV: Mrs Gorbachev.

RAISA: You understand why you must stay behind.

ZAITSEV: No.

RAISA: I understand you don't want to accept the truth.
I promise you we are moving forward.
Be patient, Slava.
*(She pushes his pink pocket square down until it is no longer
seen.)*
Next.

ZAITSEV: What?

RAISA: Show me more.

*(ZAITSEV walks over to the bed and picks up the most
beautiful of fabrics. He stands by the bed and shows it to
RAISA. She smiles.)*

RAISA: Beautiful.

(Shift)

Scene 14

*(The President's bedroom. As is his way, he is packing his
own suitcase. Standing there is SHULTZ. He has a pad in
hand; which he refers to every so often.)*

SHULTZ: Mr President.
I just wanted a chance—
We are going to this meeting with no real sense of
what it is the General Secretary is after; but I suspect

the stakes are higher for him. I believe he's using the
Summit as a way of consolidating power and—

(REAGAN *has his back to* SHULTZ. *He is searching for one
specific shirt. When he finds it, he turns back to* SHULTZ.)

REAGAN: This man of seventy-four goes to the
Coliseum for the very first time. The tour guide takes
him to a room deep inside.
This is where the slaves dressed to fight the lions.
The old man is still curious: How does one dress to
fight lions?
Very, very slowly.

(SHULTZ *smiles. It's forced.*)

SHULTZ: Mr President, Gorbachev's choice of Eduard
Shevardnadze was a radical one.
He's a reasonable man willing to compromise. Here
then lies the problem. We must come out ahead at the
Summit without seeming to. We must win without
seeming that we did.

(REAGAN *nods yes and returns to packing.*)

REAGAN: There is one goal only.

SHULTZ: What is that?

REAGAN: I believe the way to win this game is if we get
the ratings.

SHULTZ: I'm not a Hollywood man.

REAGAN: If the ratings are high enough—if the Soviets
like what they see—they'll want more. They'll want to
come here. A Summit in Washington. That's the one
goal above all others.

(REAGAN *continues to pack.* SHULTZ *expects more but when
he doesn't get it…*)

SHULTZ: Ratings, Mr President?

REAGAN: You got that right. If he comes to America, he'll have his own press following. They will be forced to show America for what it is. The people back in the Soviet Union will get a chance to experience freedom. *(He is meticulous in the way he folds his shirts and suits. There is little in the way of difference. No two suits look different.)*

SHULTZ: You're very good at that. Packing. If that's your only suitcase—

REAGAN: We're only going to be there two days, George. When I was a spokesman for G E, I learned to make it all work. Whether it was three days or a week. One suitcase.

SHULTZ: You never say much about those days.

REAGAN: I was a salesman. Now I'm a pitchman for democracy.

SHULTZ: You've come a long way.

REAGAN: I always knew I would. With kids to support, a wife, a house, no real work coming my way. I did it. Now why is it that people have so much trouble with the American dream, George.

SHULTZ: It's a hard question to answer once you've achieved it.

REAGAN: Now that's smart but it's nonsense too. You know growing up we were poor and we knew it. We didn't have the government there to tell us we were poor. Have you ever heard of oatmeal meat? You ought to have some. Make some oatmeal, mix a little ground meat into it. Out of that comes the gravy. Flatten it all out. You've made yourself something delicious. We ate a lot of that. At the time I thought it was the most delicious thing in the world because I didn't have the government telling me it wasn't.

SHULTZ: Maybe you need to share that recipe with the American people.

REAGAN: You know what the nine most terrifying words in the English language are.

SHULTZ: I'm from the government and I'm here to help.

REAGAN: I've used that one before?

SHULTZ: A few times.

REAGAN: Should I retire it?

SHULTZ: It has its uses.

REAGAN: I'm old, George, I don't have a whole lot of new material left in me.

SHULTZ: Mr President, a thought just occurred to me. I suggest you have a private meeting with the General Secretary as soon as he arrives.
The meeting will take him by surprise.
We wouldn't put it on the schedule and no one would know about it prior.

REAGAN: What would that do?

SHULTZ: The General Secretary often travels with a leather attaché in hand—a kind of security blanket. He's a man intellectually prepared; so it is your job to cast all that aside and meet him alone. Go at him emotionally. It will be a first move. One initiated by us. Charm the man and you won't have a problem.

REAGAN: Well I think that's something I can do.

SHULTZ: Good night, Mr President. Five-thirty A M.
(He notices a book on his nightstand.)
What is this?

REAGAN: Russian history.

(SHULTZ is surprised. REAGAN has prepared himself.)
(Shift)

Scene 15

(GORBACHEV's *limo*. SHEVARDNADZE *sits next to him.*)

GORBACHEV: You know, Eduard, I'm thinking about all the Politburo members, officers, and generals who were standing in line to shake my hand as I boarded the plane to come here.

SHEVARDNADZE: I would say that was a good turnout.

GORBACHEV: These are the same men who would gladly remove me from power if I make a mistake, if I give up too much.
They want me to stop the President from going forward with S D I. Is that even possible?

SHEVARDNADZE: Of course it is.

GORBACHEV: What can I expect from a man who has spent all his life denouncing us. This man is seventy-four, Eduard. After seventy-four years men don't change.

SHEVARDNADZE: Where do you draw that line, Misha. When do you give up?
Our country has existed sixty-three years.
Is the kind of change you are looking to make still possible?

(GORBACHEV *retreats to the window.*)

SHEVARDNADZE: After all tomorrow is another day.

GORBACHEV: What do you mean to say with this?

(SHEVARDNADZE *places a piece of paper in* GORBACHEV's *lap.* GORBACHEV *examines it.*)

GORBACHEV: After all, tomorrow is another day? What is this Eduard?!

SHEVARDNADZE: These are a list of famous lines from some of the President's favorite films.

GORBACHEV: Tomorrow is another day?

SHEVARDNADZE: Gone with the Wind.

GORBACHEV: You've prepared extensively but this is ridiculous.

SHEVARDNADZE: Misha, he quotes Hollywood films to make a point or win an argument. It comes natural to him; but often he will say the line incorrectly. He is a strange man who can talk you in circles until you forget what you were discussing in the first place.

GORBACHEV: What we've got here is failure to communicate? Who's Cool Hand Luke?

SHEVARDNADZE: That's the name of the film. He may instead say: our failure to communicate is what makes us failures.

GORBACHEV: This means nothing.

SHEVARDNADZE: Read on.

GORBACHEV: Roads? Where we're going we don't need roads.

SHEVARDNADZE: Back to the Future.
He might say, We are traveling together on a road we are also paving.

GORBACHEV: And what if he misquotes a line. Why does it even matter?

SHEVARDNADZE: The more we can prepare you for the way he talks the better prepared you will be to respond.

(Beat)

GORBACHEV: I wouldn't leave this town at noon for all the tea in China.

SHEVARDNADZE: High Noon. His favorite film.
One man stands his ground while the rest of the town hides from these outlaws that are on their way. One

man against the world. In his eyes we're the outlaws
and he believes he can do it all himself. Careful not to
fall for that trap.

(Pause)

(The limo rides on quietly. Then…)

GORBACHEV: What happens when these outlaws arrive
in town? In the film? What happens?

SHEVARDNADZE: *(Surprised that* GORBACHEV *has been
listening)* He meets them face to face.

GORBACHEV: How does it end?

SHEVARDNADZE: He wins, of course. But keep in mind,
Misha, this is a Hollywood film with a Hollywood
ending. The Summit doesn't have to end that way.

(The limo arrives at its destination. An AGENT *opens the
door. A flood of camera flashes blinds us and the General
Secretary for a moment.)*

(In coat and hat, GORBACHEV *looks less like the leader of a
superpower and more a regular guy who has accidentally
just wandered off the streets.* REAGAN *comes bouncing
down the stairs looking more like a man of 50 and not
74. In spite of the cold temperature, he only wears a suit.*
GORBACHEV, *not a tall man to begin with, is made even
smaller by* REAGAN's *height.)*

REAGAN: General Secretary.

GORBACHEV: Mr President.

REAGAN: It's very good to finally meet.

GORBACHEV: I have looked forward to this trip. It will
be good to sit down at the table after so many years of
silence.

REAGAN: We have two long days ahead of us, but
there's a lot we can do.

GORBACHEV: I agree.

REAGAN: Let's get to it.

(By now GORBACHEV *and* REAGAN *are at the top of the stairs.)*

REAGAN: I believe they'd like one more picture, General Secretary.

*(*REAGAN *is already turning* GORBACHEV *to face the cameras. The President does this with incredible ease.)*

*(*REAGAN waves while GORBACHEV holds on tightly to his fedora with one hand, a small wave with his other hand.

REAGAN: Are you ready?

*(*GORBACHEV *is and he isn't.)*

(One more wave and…)

END OF ACT ONE

ACT TWO

Scene 1

(We pick up right on the handshake.)

REAGAN: General Secretary.

GORBACHEV: Mr President.

REAGAN: It's very good to finally meet.

GORBACHEV: I have looked forward to this trip. It will be good to sit down at the table after so many years of silence.

REAGAN: We have two long days ahead of us, but there's a lot we can do.

GORBACHEV: I agree.

REAGAN: Let's get to it.

(By now GORBACHEV and REAGAN are at the top of the stairs.)

REAGAN: I believe they'd like one more picture, General Secretary.

(REAGAN is already turning GORBACHEV to face the cameras. The President does this with incredible ease.)

(REAGAN waves while GORBACHEV holds on tightly to his fedora with one hand, a small wave with his other hand.)

REAGAN: Are you ready?

(Shift)

Scene 2

(A small, crowded hallway. A group of advisors. The tight quarters make it impossible to tell the two sides apart.)

(We are joining a slightly heated conversation.)

(GORBACHEV is to the side taking off his heavy coat, scarf, etc.)

SHEVARDNADZE: This private meeting you're suggesting is not on the schedule.

SHULTZ: We can amend the schedule.

SHEVARDNADZE: A schedule is not amended.

SHULTZ: But of course it is. It's the way things should be done.

SHEVARDNADZE: Not in our country.

REAGAN: Boys, it's just an idea. Nothing more.

SHEVARDNADZE: But it's not in the schedule, Mr President.

REAGAN: It just occurred to me that two people meeting for the first time should spend a few minutes alone together.

SHEVARDNADZE: I would have to discuss this with my associates.

SHULTZ: And we would have wasted two days.

SHEVARDNADZE: Why don't we add this to the schedule later but for now continue as planned.

(Pause)

GORBACHEV: Thirty minutes. No more.

REAGAN: Sometimes that's all it takes.

SHULTZ: We'll adjust the schedule accordingly.

SHEVARDNADZE: I approve that the schedule be adjusted.

Now where is this meeting.

REAGAN: I'm afraid it's just us two.

SHEVARDNADZE: But that is not reasonable.

REAGAN: General Secretary when you meet someone for the first time it's smart to not have the whole family there standing over you wondering if this is going to lead to marriage.

GORBACHEV: We will meet alone.

REAGAN: This's a good start, boys. We have our first agreement.
Tell the Mississippi Catfish to get the word out.

(GORBACHEV *looks at* SHEVARDNADZE *as if to say, What the hell did he just say?*)

(Shift)

Scene 3

*(*RAISA *and* NANCY. *A small table with coffee, tea, pastries.)*

(They smile at the photographers [us]. After several flashes they are alone.)

RAISA: Siberia.

NANCY: Really. Siberia.

RAISA: Yes. Siberia. It is vacation destination for many.

NANCY: Vacation in Siberia?

RAISA: Yes.

NANCY: Oh but I've heard it's so cold there.

RAISA: I believe you will like our country very much.

NANCY: It would be nice to visit Moscow.

RAISA: But also Siberia. In the center is a special place. Lake Baikal. It is a rift lake. Do you understand what a rift lake is.

NANCY: *(To us)* I let her explain. I smiled. We had another fifty-five minutes to go.

RAISA: It is sinking of land all around because of something…
The words now fail me. Ah. Yes. Extensional tectonics. Do you understand?

NANCY: Very interesting.

RAISA: *(To us)* She had no clue.

RAISA: It is a freshwater lake bigger than the Great Lakes combined. The water is very clear.

NANCY: You must come to visit our country. Each Spring in Washington you can see the cherry blossoms but they don't last long. A week. You must visit at just the right time.

(RAISA motions a K G B AGENT over and whispers in his ear.)

NANCY: Is everything okay?

RAISA: No.

(The K G B AGENT finds a different chair and switches it with the one RAISA is sitting in.)

RAISA: The chair was uncomfortable.

NANCY: Is that better?

RAISA: Yes.

NANCY: Would you like coffee?

RAISA: Tea.

(NANCY pours her the tea.)

RAISA: A tea bag. How curious.

NANCY: How so?

RAISA: Tea leaves need room to expand if it is to release all flavors. What you are doing is drowning leaves in boiling water and flavor has no way to escape.

NANCY: *(To us)* Neither did I.

RAISA: It is just physics. I learned all about this in my first year at Moscow University in 1952. This is why we use a large samovar. The tea leaves are very strong; so you only use a small amount. You then dilute the tea with hot water for just the right taste. We use wood or acorns to heat the water and it stays just warm enough for you to be able to enjoy tea half the day.

NANCY: We have electricity. Did you encounter traffic?

RAISA: Traffic?

NANCY: You were fifteen minutes late.

RAISA: There was no traffic.

NANCY: Oh.

RAISA: There is so much happening.

NANCY: Yes, a lot to do in two days.

RAISA: I agree. Did I already apologize for being late?

NANCY: You did not.
(She looks at us with a painful smile.)
(RAISA turns back to the K G B AGENT and whispers in his ear.)

NANCY: What's the matter now?

RAISA: I do not like this chair. It is more uncomfortable.

NANCY: I sure hope they find you something comfortable before we run out of time.

RAISA: I hope too. I would not want to end this pleasant conversation because of a chair.

(NANCY *just smiles.*)

(*By now* RAISA *is sitting on a new chair.*)

RAISA: This works for me.

NANCY: Oh good.

RAISA: More countries have switched to our way of life than they have to capitalism. It sometimes seems like a one-way road we are paving.

NANCY: *(To us)* Leading to a dead end but why argue.

RAISA: I received a gold medal for my secondary education for distinction in Marxist Philosophy. And for my doctorate I walked around the whole of Soviet Union collecting surveys to explain the state of the economy.

NANCY: *(To us)* She was relentless. I tried to imagine what she and her husband talked about in bed.

RAISA: I received the Order of Lenin before my husband did.

NANCY: *(To us)* Frightening.
(*To* RAISA)
I have two children. Patti and Ronnie.

RAISA: Your son is a ballet dancer.

NANCY: He is married.

RAISA: He is an atheist.

NANCY: He's a very nice young man with all these ideas young men have. He is finding his way.

RAISA: To where?

NANCY: Where?

RAISA: You say he is finding his way. To what destination?

NANCY: Well, you know he…he is finding his place in the world.

RAISA: It is common idea of young men in your country to want to dance ballet. How very nice.

NANCY: I've heard Russian dancers are very good.

RAISA: Indeed.

NANCY: Nureyev is Russian, correct? We were glad when he came to our country. Thank you.

RAISA: You are welcome.

NANCY: And there is this young man, Baryshnikov. We are happy to have him too. There is an American expression I am sure someone who has received the Order of Stalin is familiar with.

RAISA: Lenin. Order of Lenin.

NANCY: Someone who has received Order of Lenin must be familiar with the American expression, Your loss is our gain.

RAISA: *(To us)* There is also an American expression. Bitch.

NANCY: I am also stepmother to my son Michael and my daughter Maureen.

RAISA: She is on her third marriage, correct?

NANCY: Yes, one doesn't always get it right the first time.

RAISA: Your husband did not.

NANCY: He got it right.

RAISA: Eventually.

NANCY: He got it right.

RAISA: I like to listen to Simon and Garfunkel. They separated but now are friends again. They did a concert together in your Central Park. It shows us anything is possible.

NANCY: I remember hearing about that.

RAISA: "I'd rather be a sparrow than a snail."

"I'd rather be a hammer than a nail."

The Soviet Union has sickle and hammer on its flag.

Do you believe Simon and Garfunkel is in favor of communism.

NANCY: *(To us)* Just say no. But I couldn't. She would insist on explaining her reasoning.

RAISA: Did you hear my question?

NANCY: Oh my. We're out of time.

RAISA: Already?

(To us)

If God existed this is the point I would thank Him.

NANCY: *(To us)* Thank you, God.

RAISA: *(To NANCY)* Oh this has been wonderful. I am grateful for your generous offerings.

NANCY: I look forward to continuing our conversation.

RAISA: Yes, I will host and I will make sure the seats are comfortable.

NANCY: *(To us)* Bitch.

(NANCY and RAISA turn to us and smile. Flash photography)

(Shift)

Scene 4

(Out in the grounds. SHULTZ *and* SHEVARDNADZE*)*

SHULTZ: *(To us)* The President and the General
Secretary had been in the room thirty-five minutes.

SHEVARDNADZE: *(To us)* Forty.

SHULTZ: *(To us)* Fifty-five. A nervous Eduard walked
over to me. What did he want to talk about?

SHEVARDNADZE: The weather.

SHULTZ: What?

SHEVARDNADZE: It is not cold for your President. He
did not wear coat.

SHULTZ: He is warm-blooded.

SHEVARDNADZE: Ah.
(A moment…)
Should we go in, George?

SHULTZ: And do what?

SHEVARDNADZE: The schedule has already been
adjusted once.

SHULTZ: It's possible they've come to some kind of
agreement.

SHEVARDNADZE: It is also possible this is ending
before—

*(*SHEVARDNADZE *pointing* SHULTZ *in the opposite
direction)*

SHEVARDNADZE: Looks like we have company.

SHULTZ: Oh boy.

*(*REPORTERS *swarm around* SHEVARDNADZE *and* SHULTZ*.)*

GERMAN REPORTER: Herr Shultz, why has the official
schedule been changed.

SHULTZ: I suspect the President wanted to have some alone time with the General Secretary.

SWISS REPORTER: Is it our beautiful country that has allowed them to become friends so quickly?

SHULTZ: They didn't know one another prior to today; so they were never enemies. But it is a beautiful country.

FRENCH REPORTER: And what was their intention?

SHULTZ: Excuse me?

FRENCH REPORTER: What are they discussing?

SHULTZ: We can't tell you what that is because we ourselves don't know.

AMERICAN REPORTER #1: Are you saying this was not planned by the President?

SHULTZ: That's a good question.

SHEVARDNADZE: *(To us)* He was good. I stood a step back because the closest I had come to seeing this was when interrogating an already guilty man.

BRITISH REPORTER: Minister Shevardnadze, does the General Secretary suffer from a short man complex?

SHEVARDNADZE: Excuse me?

BRITISH REPORTER: We have it on good source that he wears elevator shoes.

SHEVARDNADZE: George?

SHULTZ: *(To* BRITISH REPORTER*)* No comment.

BRITISH REPORTER: Care to elaborate?

SHULTZ: No comment.

AMERICAN REPORTER #2: Mr Shevardnadze, what does the General Secretary believe will come from these talks.

SHEVARDNADZE: No comment.

(The REPORTERS *continue to raise their hands.)*

SHEVARDNADZE: No comment.

SHULTZ: *(To us)* For a first-timer he was good.

SHEVARDNADZE: I will have to check on that.

SHULTZ: *(To us)* There's a special talent that sometimes takes years to master.

SHEVARDNADZE: We're not ready to discuss that at this moment.

SHULTZ: *(To us)* The ability of seeming to say something while not saying anything.

SHEVARDNADZE: We are here and they are in there. I just don't know.

SHULTZ: *(To us)* He was a natural at it.

SHEVARDNADZE: Good question. Next.
No.
No comment.
No comment.
No. Comment.

(The REPORTERS *go.)*

SHEVARDNADZE: Those were the most exhausting five minutes of my life.

SHULTZ: It's what happens when you have a free press. You'll get better at it when the time comes.

SHEVARDNADZE: When what time comes. Free press? I like you, George, but understand this. We are not on the same side.

SHULTZ: I'm aware of that.

SHEVARDNADZE: So when you bring up a free press.

SHULTZ: It was not my intention to—

SHEVARDNADZE: Your free press.

This is all fine when the market is divided into a thousand different voices all willing to have their individual say. But what if one company owned a few different newspapers. Would they compete with each other or would they have one single point of view? Later these companies would buy more and more newspapers or force others out of business. This process would happen slowly. No one notices it. But then suddenly one day the American people wake up and they are reading something not all too different from Pravda.

We have one newspaper and yes, it prints lies. Many lies.

But our whole country is aware of it. They are not stupid. They know they can't trust the printed word. Your country—I warn you. You have no idea where you're headed. It has happened in England. Two words: Rupert Murdoch. He has accomplished something the Soviet people have not.

He has turned lie into truth.

(Beat)

SHEVARDNADZE: Well, George. What do you say?

SHULTZ: No comment.

SHEVARDNADZE: Do not try to sell our people on a flawed system.

It is one thing to be friends but it's another to force your views on us.

As Americans say, I am no spring chicken.

(He starts to go.)

SHULTZ: *(Pointing off into the distance)* Near the lake, is that your granddaughter?

(SHEVARDNADZE turns to look.)

SHEVARDNADZE: Sopho. I brought her with me.

SHULTZ: Your expectations are high.

SHEVARDNADZE: Why do you say that?

SHULTZ: You want her to be here when history happens—if it does.

SHEVARDNADZE: I am babysitting, George.
Her parents have travelled to Paris, and my wife is taking care of the other grandchildren.
But yes.
If history does happen then I would want her to be here.

SHULTZ: How many grandchildren do you have?

SHEVARDNADZE: Five.

SHULTZ: She's your favorite.

SHEVARDNADZE: I would like to say no.
I would like to say they are all my favorite. But I would be lying to myself. We must have a favorite because when a choice is not made by you then you become a little less of what you are.

SHULTZ: You're going to have to help me there, Eduard.

SHEVARDNADZE: We are the sum of all our choices.
We choose who to love. We choose who to marry. We choose who to support. We choose our friends.
We choose our enemies. We choose our way of life.
Capitalism. Communism.
To say we don't choose our favorite grandchild is to fool yourself or to lie.
I am not a liar.

(Beat)

SHEVARDNADZE: You ever box a kangaroo.

SHULTZ: Box a kangaroo. An actual one?

SHEVARDNADZE: A man with a tattoo on his ass is likely to have done a lot of things.

SHULTZ: I'm open to it.

SHEVARDNADZE: You will lose. They are mean, George. They will beat you to death.

SHULTZ: Kangaroos?

SHEVARDNADZE: The early Fifties. A group of young Americans sat around a bar to try vodka for the first time. An Australian guy happened to be there watching. One by one the Americans all ended up on the ground. The Australian man, he said, I haven't seen something like that since my cousin got kicked by a kangaroo. The bartender picked up on that and named it the kangaroo kicker.

SHULTZ: You make that up?

SHEVARDNADZE: A good story is a good story. Ask your President.

(He goes.)

Scene 5

(The private meeting is in progress.)

(GORBACHEV and REAGAN are in a room alone. Two note-takers and two interpreters stand by to the side. We don't have to see them if we don't care to.)

(A table with a pitcher of water and some glasses. GORBACHEV is sitting down but REAGAN is near the window looking out.)

GORBACHEV: Mr President, something you said in the hallway has been on my mind this last hour. Before we continue our conversation. I believe I need clarity.

REAGAN: You may be asking the wrong person but I'll do my best.

GORBACHEV: What is a Mississippi Catfish?

REAGAN: Oh well that's our press secretary.

GORBACHEV: Mississippi catfish?

REAGAN: Larry Speakes is a polite Southern fella but you don't handle him right and you'll get horned.

GORBACHEV: That clarifies nothing.

REAGAN: I have counted seventy-three cameras. They really do want something to happen. Do you believe that's possible.

(GORBACHEV *nods.*)

REAGAN: General Secretary, let us return to this question of trust. I may not have made this clear at the start of our conversation but I want to be clear now. The American people do not like war. They hate war. America is too good a place to be when there is no war.

GORBACHEV: Mr President, the Soviet people have great respect for everything your country has accomplished. We wish you no harm.

REAGAN: Before leaving for my trip here I visited a third grade classroom. A young girl presented me with a drawing. Well I couldn't make sense of it. The paper was blank. It was soon explained to me I was looking at the wrong side. On one side there was nothing but on the other was the drawing of a handshake.

(*A moment where* GORBACHEV *wonders if there is more. There is.*)

REAGAN: That little girl showed me both possibilities even if she didn't realize it. A blank page. Nothing. Or peace.

GORBACHEV: I also find young people anxious about where we are headed. Older citizens wonder if they will once again be witness to the terrors they experienced forty-five years ago. Our people do not like war. The Soviet Union is too good a place to be when there is no war.

REAGAN: Good. We are in agreement.

GORBACHEV: *(Ignoring* REAGAN; *staying on script)* I want to say two things if you would allow me. We have had conflicts both openly and privately with regards to developing countries. There is great hunger, illiteracy, and disease in these countries. We need to help these countries. We need to take a new political approach to these issues in order to resolve them. This is our approach to foreign policy.

REAGAN: Well if you would let me respond.
We could help these developing countries; but the United States feels that your attempt to help is really a guise for using force to shape the fate of these countries.
To have these countries conform to your beliefs.
Often these beliefs of yours are shared only by a small group of people in the country. Let these different factions settle their differences themselves. Only when these internal differences have been solved should we assist them in improving their economies.

(Beat)

GORBACHEV: It is clear to me there is much to discuss.

REAGAN: You had two things to say. Go on.

GORBACHEV: I have received some news that should be of grave concern to you. Our scientists are convinced that there will be a great earthquake in the area of California and Nevada within the next three years with a magnitude of seven or seven-point-five on the Richter scale. We are prepared to give you a full report of our findings as a gesture of good will.

REAGAN: Thank you for this information but we are aware of it.

Our scientists have advised me that such an event is long overdue because of faults in the Earth and shifting plates.

There is great tension that has not been released. It is, as you say, a matter of time. But there is always that one chance that it will not happen.

GORBACHEV: You are resigned.

REAGAN: To God's will. Yes.

GORBACHEV: And for those of us who do not believe in God.

(REAGAN *goes to respond but then realizes he can't.*)

(Shift)

Scene 6

(GORBACHEV *alone in his bedroom going over a set of papers. Next to him is the coat he wore at the top of the act.*)

(RAISA *is there. She writes in her journal.*)

RAISA: I've invited her to Siberia.

GORBACHEV: What did she say?

RAISA: She's packing her bags.

(Silence)

GORBACHEV: I'm wondering why I let Eduard push me into this. Nothing will happen as long as that man is in power.

RAISA: You're certain?

GORBACHEV: I meet him in a room, I talk with him for over an hour, and in the end I have no idea who he is other than someone who believes in miracles. When I warned him about a possible earthquake—

RAISA: It's in God's hands. I read the notes.

GORBACHEV: He said he was resigned. What does that even mean? He is impossible to understand—the way his mind works. Should this man be in charge of a country?

RAISA: He's won twice. Both times in a landslide.

GORBACHEV: Then I rephrase the question.
Is the United States a country whose people should have the right to vote.
There lies democracy's great flaw. Stupid people.
Stupid people running. Stupid people voting.
It's a shame.
What a great idea it would be if it weren't for all the idiots.

RAISA: I don't believe he's a total idiot.

(GORBACHEV *looks back at* RAISA.)

RAISA: You arranged for both of you to arrive to that first meeting at the same time.
You would each get out of your cars and walk toward one another. You would shake hands and walk up the stairs together. Is that right?

GORBACHEV: That was the agreement.

RAISA: He got there first.

GORBACHEV: Or I arrived late. Come. Say what you have to say.

RAISA: He made it a point to arrive early, to come down those stairs without a coat. You looked small. He looked large.

He was the host inviting you to his table.
He's not stupid, Misha, he's an actor!

(GORBACHEV *recognizes this to be true*.)

RAISA: Never wear that coat again! Throw it away. And
as long as we're here never wear a coat period. Act like
the young man you are.

GORBACHEV: Maybe he's acting, maybe he's not, but he
said something at the top of our meeting that was odd.
He said it was us.
Me. Him. We were the only two people capable of
solving this problem. He never went into the how. No
details. Nothing. It was us. We both had roles to play.

RAISA: Roles?

GORBACHEV: There was a sign I saw a young woman
holding up as we drove to the meeting.
"The world does not belong only to the two of you."
Clearly the world does not belong only to the two of
us, but when I was in the room with him he acted as if
it did.

RAISA: He's an actor, Misha! Do I have to keep
repeating myself. He's preying on your emotions.

GORBACHEV: I don't believe he was acting.

RAISA: That's the point of acting. To make you believe
he's not acting.

(*Her sudden burst of impatience gives way to compassion*.)
Misha, remember a dream you once had. Falling down
this large tunnel. I was there too. There was light but it
was disappearing as shadows started to come over us.

GORBACHEV: That dream was so long ago.

RAISA: Thirty years ago and both of us remember it.
Why? Those shadows never go away, I know you feel
as if you're falling, but that dream of yours does not
have us disappearing into the darkness. The light is

there. It's always there. Misha, what dreams rarely give us is an ending. Dreams reveal the truth but they don't tell us what to do with it. How you want that dream to end—it's up to you.

GORBACHEV: I understand.

RAISA: He has a nice smile—the President does—but iron teeth. Next time you meet with him put all your papers, your notes aside. Start acting. Play the leading man the world expects you to be. Push this man off the stage if you have to.

(Shift)

Scene 7

(The negotiating room. REAGAN, SHULTZ, *and* SHEVARDNADZE *are there along with* AIDES *who listen, take notes, but do not speak.* GORBACHEV, *standing, has a temper; which flares up every so often. This is the emotion at the top of the scene.)*

GORBACHEV: It is ridiculous to go almost seven years without meeting face to face. This point must be made clear to everyone in this room but also in your country.

SHULTZ: General Secretary, if you would to the table.

GORBACHEV: The whole business of using newspapers and television to talk to one another is ridiculous. Every day my advisors read your newspapers looking for your words and the real meaning behind them. Words meant for me.

REAGAN: General Secretary, I'm not as smart as you or your advisors make me out to be.

GORBACHEV: Enough! Our relationship is not a good one. Your most recent statements indicate that you want improved relations.

SHULTZ: That's correct.

(GORBACHEV *sits and grabs a piece of paper from advisor.*)

GORBACHEV: But not even a year ago, you say this on national radio. And I quote, "My fellow Americans, I'm pleased to announce I've just signed legislation that will outlaw the Soviet Union forever. We begin bombing in five minutes."

SHULTZ: That recording was made during a sound check. It was not meant to be heard by anyone.

GORBACHEV: A joke?

SHULTZ: Yes.

GORBACHEV: It was a joke?! That joke could have set off a nuclear war. Now tell me this, Mr President, who are we to believe? The man who said those words or the one who sits now across from me assuring us he wants peace. You are two different people. You must be one if there is to be trust.

Who are you?

Who are you, Mr President?

REAGAN: It is clear that there has been a failure to communicate.

This is the first meeting where our two superpowers have sat down with the hope of reducing arms. Yet over the last few years we have seen a Soviet military buildup. We have fewer nuclear weapons than in 1969. You have five-point-four million men in your armed forces; we have half the amount.

SHEVARDNADZE: (*To us*) He was just making up numbers!

REAGAN: Americans want televisions and those videocassette recorders that have become so popular. That's the basic interest of our industry. Not bombs. Americans buy cars and planes.

SHEVARDNADZE: *(To us)* Planes? That is exactly what he said. Americans buy planes.

REAGAN: Our budget for humanitarian affairs. For those who need help. Our elderly and handicapped and other social needs is greater than our military budget.

SHULTZ: *(To us)* Statistics. The President was going into uncharted waters.

(To everyone in the room)

I suggest we take a half hour break.

(All eyes are on GORBACHEV *now.)*

GORBACHEV: We will take a half hour break.

(They all rise from the table.)

(Time passes.)

Scene 8

(They all sit down and once again we join them in mid-conversation.)

REAGAN: Please don't take this the wrong way.

GORBACHEV: It was our responsibility to support a people who had freely chosen a change of government.

REAGAN: You invaded Afghanistan. As a way to force socialist ideas on a country that had no interest.

GORBACHEV: No. NO! They asked for our help.
They chose the road they wanted to travel. But then turned to us for help. They said, Roads? Where we're going we don't have roads. Help.

SHEVARDNADZE: *(To us)* Things were taking a strange turn. It was now the General Secretary appropriating and misquoting American films.

SHULTZ: *(To us)* I believed it was from a movie I had seen recently with my nephew. I couldn't recall the title, but it was about a young man who went back to the past, and then back to the future.

GORBACHEV: We want nothing more than to leave Afghanistan.

REAGAN: That is what we want too. You have helped them pave the road now let them go forward into the future and not back.

SHULTZ: *(To us)* Let me add. I did not care for the film. It used incest as the basis for comedy. Appalling.

GORBACHEV: The Soviet Union supports a political settlement, overseen by the United Nations, for an independent Afghanistan and Soviet troop withdrawal. Yet you won't back it because you want us there. You want us to continue to carry that expense.

(REAGAN looks to SHULTZ and his aides. A moment)

REAGAN: We're willing to back the mutual withdrawal of all outside forces and help supervise the installation of a government chosen by the people of Afghanistan. Do I have your promise, General Secretary, to reach this end?

(GORBACHEV motions to his aides who gather around him and they discuss briefly in quiet.)

GORBACHEV: Our aides will work on a proposal that satisfies both our needs. But, Mr President, the press cannot be told of this agreement until the proper time. I do not want our young men in Afghanistan to find this out from Radio Free Europe. Be patient.

REAGAN: I will follow your lead, but your withdrawal must be complete within the next two years. If you have not left Afghanistan after that...

(He realizes something.)

Well, I don't need to finish that idea, because…I trust you.

GORBACHEV: Then Mr President, I would like to address the main issue that has brought us here. S D I. The Strategic Defense Initiative.

SHULTZ: Maybe we should take another break.

SHEVARDNADZE: Is the President not feeling well? I suggest we continue.

SHULTZ: Let's stop for now.

REAGAN: Hold on, George. Gentlemen.

SHULTZ: Mr President.

REAGAN: General Secretary, will you take a private walk with me. There's a boat house by the lake. Let's continue our talk there.

SHEVARDNADZE: General Secretary, may I speak with you.

(GORBACHEV waves SHEVARDNADZE off.)

(Shift)

Scene 9

(The men are walking the grounds.)

REAGAN: I know your analysts may tell you otherwise but I was not just a B-list actor.

GORBACHEV: Mr President, it would be foolish on our part to spend valuable resources discussing your films.

REAGAN: But you have.

GORBACHEV: Not just discuss but they made me watch them.

REAGAN: That's terrible. I am so sorry.

GORBACHEV: Some I didn't enjoy.

REAGAN: I respect your honesty.

GORBACHEV: Many I didn't finish.

REAGAN: Good for you. I was told you were a smart man. It's clear you are.

(Beat)

GORBACHEV: Mr President, I believe *Kings Row* to be a very good film.

REAGAN: I'll take whatever compliment you give me.

GORBACHEV: There is a very famous line: "Where is the rest of me?"

REAGAN: General Secretary, I believe you missed your true calling.

GORBACHEV: There is the final moment where you are told the truth. Your friend reveals you have been the victim of a sadistic doctor. The news should break your heart.
The truth should destroy you. Those who love you most are afraid of what the truth will do to you. But your reaction surprises them as much as it does your audience.
You smile.
You laugh.
The truth has finally freed you.
You laugh and you declare your intent to move into a new house in plain daylight for everyone to see you.
You want to throw a party and invite everyone.
It is your best performance, Mr President, because it is not a performance.
It is you. You are an optimist. This is why you're here.
It is not me.

(Beat)

REAGAN: I noticed there is a pool house on the property. Why don't we go there.

(Shift)

Scene 10

(A small living room. NANCY is there.)

(SHULTZ enters.)

NANCY: Good afternoon, George.

SHULTZ: An aide said you wanted to have a private conversation.

NANCY: Now why do they have to go and make it all sound so ominous. As if you were in some trouble and needed—

SHULTZ: I didn't believe I was in trouble.

NANCY: Oh well good. Good.
You have a moment?

SHULTZ: Yes.

NANCY: George, there have been some rumblings in the press about...well a teabag. There's this whole business about whether I was wrong to use a teabag and why the tea—
Well I'll let you speak.

(Beat)

SHULTZ: A teabag?

NANCY: Yes.

SHULTZ: Is this about your tea with Mrs Gorbachev?

NANCY: The press can be so critical.
How do you feel about teabags?

SHULTZ: It's a funny thing. I've never given it much thought.

NANCY: Prince Charles visited the White House and I used teabags. Now if it's good enough for Prince Charles then it should be good enough for Mrs Gorbachev.

SHULTZ: I don't believe the press corps is too concerned about whether a teabag was used or not.

NANCY: The press writes what they have to write but what I really want to know. What will you say about it? The teabag.

SHULTZ: Mrs Reagan, I have no intention—

NANCY: When it comes time to write your memoirs.

SHULTZ: It's not something I've thought about.

NANCY: Everyone does it. You will too. I have it on good source.

SHULTZ: You do?

NANCY: My friend in California. She knows.

SHULTZ: Can you ask her what kind of advance I should expect?

NANCY: You have a good sense of humor, George. No more about a teabag; so I don't expect you to mention it.

SHULTZ: Of course not.

(Beat)

NANCY: George, you spend a lot of time with my husband. What do you know about him?

SHULTZ: That's a broad question.

NANCY: My husband is a man whose father was an alcoholic. A man whose parents moved around a great deal. This made it hard for him to find lifelong friends. If you move often, George, you find it difficult to let people in because, ultimately, you know any new friends are really just strangers who you will likely never see again.

SHULTZ: I am not a stranger to him.

NANCY: I know.

(Beat)

If it's any consolation let me tell you something that I haven't told many people. I've known Ronnie a long time—thirty-three years we've been married—but there is a wall around him. I've come closest to getting past it but I know I haven't. Not really.

SHULTZ: This is not about a teabag, is it?

NANCY: I wish I knew more. I see him tell a story to a group of people. It's a story he's told before but now it has changed. And I wonder which is the real one or if it even happened. Maybe it's all a performance.

SHULTZ: He loves you very much.

NANCY: I know that.

(Pause)

SHULTZ: Mrs Reagan, I spoke to your husband a few weeks after the attempt on his life. It was one of those conversations that…well there was no one thing on the agenda. It was free-flowing, which made it unusual. Somehow we ended up talking about our youth. His time as a lifeguard. The number of people he saved from drowning during that time…the number has only grown. I jokingly pointed this out, and he got very serious. More serious than I have ever seen him be. He talked about how close he came to death, about the young man who shot him…you see, I didn't know what he was saying. And then he brought it all back to his time as a lifeguard. The reason the number grows is because it's true. I had no idea what to say to that. And then he said something else. The number isn't large enough yet. "I have saved too few lives, but the summer isn't over. And that's why God spared me."

NANCY: It's a wonderful story. One I haven't heard. And because I haven't heard it a second or third time, I believe it is true. He gave you a gift, George.

SHULTZ: I believe so.

(Beat)

NANCY: On your way out, please tell an aide to make sure the heat is on in the car.

(SHULTZ goes. NANCY is left alone. After a few seconds…)

NANCY: *(Smiles)* A lifeguard.
Oh, Ronnie.

(Shift)

Scene 11

(GORBACHEV sits on a couch in the pool house watching a film. REAGAN stokes a fire.)

(In his body language, it is clear GORBACHEV is bored, frustrated, impatient, maybe even angry. He explodes:)

GORBACHEV: Mr President. Please. There is only so much time. We can't waste it continuing to watch this movie.

REAGAN: Shhh.

GORBACHEV: I have been patient but this—

REAGAN: Listen carefully to this last part.

(GORBACHEV and REAGAN listen. It's important that lines in bold pop, but the sound isn't perfect.)

TELEVISION: You will forgive me if I speak bluntly. **The universe grows smaller** every day; and the threat of **aggression by any group anywhere can no longer be** tolerated. **There must be security for all or no one** is secure. **This does not mean giving up any freedom except the freedom to act irresponsibly.** We of the other planets have long accepted this principle. I came here to give you the facts. It is **no concern of ours how you run your own** planet—but **if you threaten to extend your violence, this Earth of yours will be reduced to a burned-out cinder.**

(REAGAN *hits pause.*)

(*Lights on* SHEVARDNADZE)

SHEVARDNADZE: *(To us)* An odd moment in history that was not planned.

(*Lights on* SHULTZ)

SHULTZ: *(To us)* In fact it was. Matches. Kindling. Dry wood. Comfortable chairs. A pitcher of water. A T V, V C R with a copy of *The Day the Earth Stood Still* inside it. A day earlier the President and his wife took a walk on the grounds.

When the President saw the abandoned pool house, he decided to set the stage for what he referred to me as humanity's last hope. I thought the statement was a little too grand, but he's an actor and one must allow for some of that.

(SHEVARDNADZE *and* SHULTZ *disappear.*)

REAGAN: Did you enjoy the film?

GORBACHEV: Very compelling.

REAGAN: That was Michael Rennie. A British actor.

GORBACHEV: We can discuss the film at dinner but there are some other issues—

REAGAN: I auditioned for it. If you're curious, I didn't get the part.

GORBACHEV: Mr President, I'm sorry you did not get to
play an alien—

REAGAN: A warning has been given and us two are
the ones who can hear it. Call it what you will. God or
Michael Rennie, but we've been warned.

(Beat)

You don't see it, do you?

Mr Gorbachev, do you believe there is life on other
planets?

GORBACHEV: Sure.

REAGAN: And are they our friends?

GORBACHEV: I don't know because I haven't met them
yet.

REAGAN: Let's say they're not.

GORBACHEV: If you insist.

REAGAN: If these other-world visitors attack us would
your country step forward and help us.

GORBACHEV: But in this movie you showed me there's
no attack. Mr President, you are very confused.

REAGAN: Will you help us?

GORBACHEV: *(Bewildered)* Of course.

REAGAN: We would do the same. Whatever our
disagreements may be, we would figure out a way
of helping one another, but why wait for that outside
force to arrive.
Let's settle all our differences now.

GORBACHEV: Mr President, we have come here with
the hope of halting the arms race. We want to deal
seriously with disarmament. But if that is truly the case
then answer this. What is the purpose of deploying a
weapon—

REAGAN: We have no intention of using the Strategic Defense Initiative as an offensive weapon.

GORBACHEV: A shield?

REAGAN: Yes a shield. With S D I in place nuclear weapons will become useless.

GORBACHEV: If you were to create this shield then we would no longer be working under the principal idea of mutual assured destruction. And without mutual assured destruction you could—in theory—launch a nuclear strike without fearing retaliation. You would be protected and the balance of power will shift in ways that are unacceptable.

REAGAN: We would never launch a first strike.

GORBACHEV: How can I trust you on that? How will I explain to my grandchildren, as the missiles fly under some future president, that President Reagan asked me to trust him?

REAGAN: Once this technology is in place we will share it with you.

GORBACHEV: Will you also give us the capital to build it? As you see, the variables are too great, Mr President. I ask you to stop and really examine what you're doing before going forward.

REAGAN: If my men were to draft a treaty—

GORBACHEV: With all respect, I do not believe treaties. In the end they are always broken.
Realize this, Mr President, we are mortal. Whether the technology is in place two years from now or ten, we can't guarantee that either one of us will be around to enforce this promise. In three years-time you will have no power. As for me, it can be a year or twenty, but promises made by mortals do not last.
(Beat)

If you go forward with S D I and we learn you're months away from achieving that technology…when that time comes. If.

Mr President, we would have no choice left…

I am sorry to paint such a grim picture of the future, but you must face the reality of the present.

(Beat)

No nuclear weapons; no S D I. It's that simple. The choice is yours.

(Pause)

REAGAN: Mr Gorbachev, we must accept that we are not going to reach an agreement today. But the world is running out of time. I'd like to invite you to visit Washington next Spring.

GORBACHEV: We can discuss any future negotiations another time.

REAGAN: If we are to give the world some hope we must come out of this Summit closer to an agreement than when we arrived.

Will you accept my invitation?

(Beat)

GORBACHEV: I must give this thought. You will have my response soon.

REAGAN: Why are you hesitating.

GORBACHEV: You don't make a decision like this without first asking the family.

(Shift)

Scene 12

(RAISA *escorts* NANCY *showing her paintings made by children.*)

NANCY: I'm sorry I was late. For some reason, my driver could not find the Soviet Embassy. It's a little out of the way.

RAISA: It depends what way you take.

NANCY: Well I am so sorry.

RAISA: I expected nothing less.

NANCY: What was that?

RAISA: Her name is right under. Sasha Khrebtukova. And this is her age.

NANCY: She is seven?

RAISA: That's right.
Over here. Yuri Gagarin. First man in space.
And over here. Come. This young talented Soviet boy is only five.

NANCY: Very nice.

RAISA: That is Red Square during a little parade we have every year.

NANCY: What is the celebration?

RAISA: The birth of communism.

NANCY: But all those missiles.
You have too many of them.

RAISA: I believe if he were to draw your entire nuclear arsenal he would need a bigger piece of paper.

NANCY: Hmm.

RAISA: Missiles can destroy the world.

NANCY: *(To us)* Here we go again.

RAISA: A nuclear missile from Turkey can reach Red Square in less than ten minutes. That is a nightmare for all children.

The death of the world.

Let's have tea.

(Shift)

(Another room)

(Tea. Samovar. Fancy)

NANCY: *(To us)* Earlier that day, Ronnie had assigned me the joyless job of inviting the Gorbachevs to Washington.

That way, at the very least, we would come out ahead.

RAISA: It would be wonderful to have you come to Moscow.

(To us)

My task was to have the Reagans come to Moscow first.

Misha wanted to come out ahead.

RAISA/ NANCY: *(To us)*The things we do for our husbands.

RAISA: When you come to Moscow you must bring your ballet-dancing son, so he can see the great Moscow Ballet.

NANCY: He's married.

RAISA: Then bring spouse.

NANCY: I will tell him.

RAISA: Do so.

(NANCY smiles.)

NANCY: I have some good news.
When you come to America I will arrange for you to meet Simon and Garfunkel.

RAISA: You bring them with you to Moscow.

NANCY: You come to Washington and meet them.

RAISA: After Moscow.

NANCY: Before.

RAISA: After.

NANCY: Before.

RAISA: After.

(Beat)

NANCY: Why don't we have tea. I wouldn't want us to run out of time.

RAISA: It is a great tradition we hold on to.
When relatives and even friends are no longer speaking to one another they meet for tea. A samovar between them.
Then they talk to the samovar not each other. For example.
Dear Samovar, explain to this woman before me the value of peace. Then it would be the other person's turn.
After an hour the two would once again be on talking terms.

NANCY: *(To us)* Dear Samovar, save me now from having to hear her talk for another hour.

(RAISA *pours the tea out.*)

RAISA: The tea is very strong; so you put a small amount.
Now you can dilute the tea with hot water for just the right taste.

NANCY: And they have this in every Soviet home.

RAISA: Yes. A larger one.

A small teapot such as the one you used just says
you're selfish and greedy and don't care about others.
But I know that was not your intention. How do you
like the tea?

NANCY: Very good.

RAISA: And these are just a few pastries.
This is my favorite.
It translates to Birds' Milk Cake. Try some.

NANCY: It is made with birds' milk?

RAISA: Of course not.

NANCY: It's very good whatever it is.
(To us)
I was trying hard.
She then started up again with the great virtues of
communism.

RAISA: *(To us)* And she smiled. Clueless.
Why did my husband punish me this way.

NANCY: *(To us)* I had only one job and time was
running out.
I needed to get her and her husband to accept an
invitation to come to Washington.
(To RAISA)
I would love to address your samovar.

RAISA: Explain again.

NANCY: The Soviet traditions. The samovar.
Enemies becoming friends.
You're not my enemy but it is such a curious thing to
do.

RAISA: Go ahead.

NANCY: Dear Samovar, please ask this great woman
sitting in front of me if she would bless us all with a
trip to Washington in the Spring.

(Pause)

RAISA: Dear Samovar, tell her she must travel to
Moscow, so that she can understand our way of life.

NANCY: Dear Samovar, tell her I promise to acquaint
myself with the works of Marx and Lenin but such
work takes time.
After her trip to Washington I will more than gladly
travel to Moscow—Marx, Lenin in tow.

RAISA: Dear Samovar, tell her the Soviet people wait
for her visit.

NANCY: Dear Samovar, tell her the cherry blossoms
come in Spring. I would love to summer in Siberia.
(To us)
Now who wouldn't want that?
(To the samovar)
But I would not want her to miss the cherry blossoms,
dear Samovar.

(RAISA hesitates.)

NANCY: I'm sorry. Have I said something wrong?
Spring does come before summer, correct?

RAISA: It is very correct. Very good.
(Pause)
We will visit your great country first.

RAISA: I am happy to meet your ballet-dancer son.
(To us)
And the rest of her dysfunctional children.

*(NANCY smiles to every single one of us. She fought the war
and won.)*

(Light on SHULTZ)

SHULTZ: Diplomacy in action.
The samovar now is a museum piece for all to see.
It stands behind a glass case.

Many people believe it was this very samovar that put us on the path to end the Cold War.

(Shift)

Scene 13

(A bedroom. Two doors. One leads into the bathroom a second to a sitting room. At this moment both doors are closed. REAGAN is alone on stage. His white dress shirt is not tucked in. He is lost. NANCY enters.)

NANCY: I've decided we should arrive on time.

(Noticing REAGAN standing still)

NANCY: Why are you just standing there?

(Beat)

REAGAN: My cufflinks. I don't remember what I did with them.

NANCY: Top drawer. You put them in there.

(REAGAN finds them all the while NANCY looks in the mirror.)

NANCY: Smile. I don't remember the last time I saw you like this.

REAGAN: Darling, can you help me with these?

(NANCY walks over.)

(RAISA enters followed by GORBACHEV. The four share the same space.)

RAISA: *(Looking in mirror)* I just don't know if I should wear this.

GORBACHEV: The dress is perfect.

RAISA: You didn't say I look perfect in it.

REAGAN: I forgot to tell you just now. You look beautiful.

GORBACHEV: You are the most beautiful woman in the world.

NANCY: I believe my life didn't start until I met you.

REAGAN: You know. I'm starting to wonder.

NANCY: What's that?

REAGAN: If I could have just done it differently. Maybe I could have convinced him on S D I.

GORBACHEV: Should I have put my trust in him.

RAISA: We would return home and immediately dispatched to a dacha near the Black Sea. All hope lost.

NANCY: There is a next time. He is coming to Washington. You'll do it there.

(NANCY *exits into other room.* REAGAN *sits putting his shoes on.* GORBACHEV *is on the other side of the bed doing the same.)*

GORBACHEV: There is this American expression. You just gave away the store. I wonder if that's what I did. But then I wonder, Is there a store to give away. If we have nothing then what did I really give up.

RAISA: Our ideals remain.

GORBACHEV: And what am I to do with that?

REAGAN: "Where is the rest of me?" I nailed that line after only two takes. If I could just have a second take. A do-over.

GORBACHEV: I should have played into his emotions more.

RAISA: It's only the first step. We'll get there.

REAGAN: I still can convince him.

GORBACHEV: When we get them to stand down. If we even get that far. Then what comes next?

NANCY: *(Enters hearing* REAGAN'*s last line)* Did I just hear a hint of optimism?

REAGAN: Just a hint.

NANCY: I never doubted you.

(Suddenly they're all sitting on the bed.)

RAISA: I've been thinking the same thing, "what comes next?"

GORBACHEV: Good things for us all. I have to believe that.

RAISA: Did I just hear a hint of optimism?

GORBACHEV: Don't stand near him. It's contagious.

(Pause)

NANCY: Let's not get there late.

RAISA: Dinner.

*(*REAGAN *rises.)*

REAGAN: Dinner it is.

RAISA: I had a thought. Let them walk in first. I want them looking at us when we enter.
(She goes.)

NANCY: We will walk in first. It's the correct thing to do.
(Beat)
Ronnie.

REAGAN: What is it?

NANCY: You're not alone in this. I'm here.

REAGAN: I know that.

NANCY: What are you thinking just now?

REAGAN: I'll tell you later.

*(*REAGAN *goes followed by* NANCY.*)*

(A blow dryer is heard offstage. It startles GORBACHEV *only to realize a second later it's his wife doing her hair.)*

*(*GORBACHEV *remains sitting. Alone. Lonely)*

(Shift)

Scene 14

(A cocktail room)

*(*SHEVARDNADZE *is having a Manhattan. A moment or two,* SHULTZ *enters. A* WAITER *takes his coat.)*

SHULTZ: It's cold out there.

SHEVARDNADZE: Cold? You're a sissy, George. Sissy, is that right? Or do I have my English wrong.

SHULTZ: Sissy is fine.

SHEVARDNADZE: And you accept my insult?

SHULTZ: I have to find a way to compromise one way or other.

SHEVARDNADZE: Enough compromising. What's done is done. Grow some balls.

SHULTZ: Eduard, you are in a mood today.

*(*SHEVARDNADZE *hugs and kisses* SHULTZ *who is not used to that kind of affection.)*

SHEVARDNADZE: We did it.

SHULTZ: I suppose.

SHEVARDNADZE: We pushed them a little further up the hill.

SHULTZ: What are you drinking?

SHEVARDNADZE: A Manhattan, of course. You?

SHULTZ: A Perfect Manhattan.

SHEVARDNADZE: Now, George, why when we've become close friends do you have to go and try to show me up.

SHULTZ: It's not that mine is better than yours. A Perfect Manhattan is equal parts sweet and dry vermouth.

SHEVARDNADZE: Ah. So dry vermouth makes it perfect.

SHULTZ: It's bittersweet if you like that sort of thing.

SHEVARDNADZE: I don't.

SHULTZ: Then we both have what we want.

SHEVARDNADZE: Why are you early?

SHULTZ: You were here first.

SHEVARDNADZE: I don't like to walk into a room when everyone is here.

SHULTZ: No need to call attention to myself.

SHEVARDNADZE: Exactly.

SHULTZ: The photographers aren't even here.

SHEVARDNADZE: This is how I like it. I have my drink, then I disappear into the background.

SHULTZ: Here is to that.

(By now we have started to hear the sounds of people arriving.)

SHULTZ: As the President says each time he's about to walk out of Air Force One. It's showtime, folks.

SHEVARDNADZE: Showtime.

(Shift)

(SHULTZ and SHEVARDNADZE blend into the crowd. The REAGANS and the GORBACHEVS are there. As well as many others.)

(GORBACHEV rises, glass in hand.)

GORBACHEV: There will be no speeches here tonight.

RAISA: *(To us)* When he says that, he means it will be a very long one.

GORBACHEV: But I will like to say a few things.
I want to thank the President and his lovely wife for joining us.

SHEVARDNADZE: *(To us)* Earlier I suggested to Misha he needed to imitate the President's style; so we made up a story.

GORBACHEV: It is true that a cartoonist sent me a cartoon.
There I was on one side of the abyss and on the other stood the President. Mr President yells out, "Misha, I am prepared to go my part of the way!" At which point I say, "Go for it."

SHULTZ: *(To us)* I was impressed. The joke was right out of the President's playbook. I couldn't help but look over at where Eduard was smiling.

GORBACHEV: But that is not what happened here today.
We stood on opposite sides of the abyss. We watched each other carefully.
At some point it became clear we needed to build a bridge.
We have started construction.
It was suggested we stay in Geneva as long as necessary to resolve all questions of war and peace.
But at the rate we are going we will be here till the holidays.

REAGAN: Well if I may clarify.
I think the General Secretary meant next Christmas not the one right around the corner.

GORBACHEV: The President of the United States is correct.

(He realizes he's said something surprising.)
In my life I would never think I'd say those words. The
President of the United States is correct.
Now please raise your glasses. To the President.
To the First Lady.
To the people of the United States; whom we regard so
highly. And to these discussions and those to come.

(They drink. GORBACHEV *sits down. Now it's* REAGAN's
turn.)

REAGAN: This is a beginning.
We have failed to agree on many issues but we have
agreed on one.
The Gorbachevs will visit our country next year and at
some later time Nancy and I will travel to Moscow.
This is an auspicious night.
It was exactly forty-three years ago on this date that
the Soviet army began the counterattack at Stalingrad.
This turned the war around. Let this anniversary also
mark a turning point. One of the great leaders of the
American Revolution was Thomas Payne. He famously
said, "We have it in our power to start the world over
again." To the General Secretary and Mrs Gorbachev.
To the Soviet people. To our great nations, and the
people of this world. Peace and freedom.

(Momentary freeze. Smiles. Flash photo of SHULTZ,
SHEVARDNADZE, REAGAN, *and* GORBACHEV. *Hope frozen
in time.)*

SHULTZ: *(To us)* Next day's edition of *The New York
Times* and *Pravda* carried the exact same photograph.

SHEVARDNADZE: *(To us)* It was a first time.

(Shift)

*(*SHULTZ *is putting on his coat and getting ready to leave the
party just as* SHEVARDNADZE *enters drink in hand.)*

SHEVARDNADZE: You're leaving, George?

SHULTZ: We call it an Irish goodbye.

SHEVARDNADZE: What's that?

SHULTZ: When you leave a party without saying goodbye. Some people find it rude but others believe it's the best way to take your exit.

(Beat)

SHEVARDNADZE: Oh, let's not get too philosophical about this.

(Suddenly, SHEVARDNADZE embraces SHULTZ and kisses him. This takes the Princeton man back but he goes with it and smiles.)

SHEVARDNADZE: We did it, George!

SHULTZ: Both of us. We got them in the room together.

SHEVARDNADZE: How do you feel about the future.

SHULTZ: It may be too early but for the sake of answering your question. Optimistic.

(SHEVARDNADZE takes this in not sure whether to surrender to the optimism.)

SHEVARDNADZE: Where I'm from, Tbilisi, there are customs some people still hold on to. It is what you call an arranged marriage. The two people are pushed together by family. They meet at a restaurant, for example. Or maybe at a party. The family makes sure this happens over and over until…then comes the marriage proposal, engagement, and finally the wedding. It's all a negotiation where both families hope for the best.
(He disappears.)

(A moment later a burst of joy from the party but it doesn't last.)

(Shift)

Scene 15

(The President's ranch)

SHULTZ: *(To us)* The President was diagnosed with Alzheimer's in 1994. I visited him soon after. He was taking down a fence on his ranch.

REAGAN: You're wearing a suit, George. It's not a funeral. Just lunch.

(Beat)

How is life, George.

SHULTZ: Mr President. What are you doing?

REAGAN: *(Pointing at the fence)* Building a fence. What does it look like I'm doing?

SHULTZ: It looks to me as if you're tearing down a fence.

(Beat)

REAGAN: It's that halfway point. You can't really tell.

(Beat)

SHULTZ: I was saddened when I heard the diagnosis.

REAGAN: I can't beat this one, but I can give it a hell of a fight.

SHULTZ: If I may ask…

(REAGAN smiles.)

REAGAN: Doctors tell me to do something meaningful to me. Exercise the body and the mind.
They say to do it over and over again.
You mind handing me the hammer.

(SHULTZ hands it over.)

REAGAN: Now take that jacket off and let's get it done.

(SHULTZ takes off his jacket.)

REAGAN: One month I build a fence. The next month I take it down.

(NANCY *enters and watches* REAGAN *and* SHULTZ *work.*)

END OF PLAY